# WORLD LEADERS

## WHO SHAPED WORLD HISTORY

### Kathleen Paparchontis

**A Bluewood Book**

This edition produced and published
by Bluewood Books
A Division of The Siyeh Group, Inc.,
P.O. Box 689
San Mateo, CA 94401

ISBN 0-912517-46-8

Printed in U.S.A.
10, 9, 8, 7, 6, 5, 4, 3, 2, 1

Editor: Tony Napoli
Indexer: Kathy Paparchontis
Designer: Kevin Harris

Key to cover illustration:
Clockwise, starting from top left:
Catherine the Great, Constantine the
Great, Genghis Khan, Alfred the
Great, Vladimir Lenin, Napoleon
Bonaparte, and Franklin D. Roosevelt
in the center.

About the Author
**Kathleen Paparchontis** is a
northern California free-lance writer
and editor. She is the co-author of
Sacramento Women Past and Present
(1998), and has written a variety of
historical articles for regional publica-
tions.

Picture Acknowledgements:
All images and photos from the
Bluewood Archives; Library of
Congress, National Archives,
National Portrait Gallery, San Mateo
Public Library, United Nations and
the White House with the following
exceptions: 57: African Museum; 80:
Ben-Gurion House; 70: Chinese
Government Tourist Office; 65, 83:
French Embassy Press and
Information Division; 23: German
Information Center; 72: Imperial War
Museum; 98: Information Service of
India; 102: Mayibuye Centre; 59:
Mexican National Tourist Council;
99: Philippine Foreign Information
Service; 107: Polish Information
Agency.

# TABLE OF CONTENTS

INTRODUCTION    7

1. KHUFU    8
   (C. 2500  B.C.)

2. SARGON THE GREAT    9
   (C. 2300  B.C.)

3. HAMMURABI    10
   (C. 1792–C. 1750 B.C.)

4. KING DAVID    11
   (C. 1010–C. 970 B.C.)

5. CYRUS THE GREAT    12
   (C. 600–530 B.C.)

6. SIDDHARTHA GAUTAMA (THE BUDDHA)   13
   (C. 563–483 B.C.)

7. XERXES I    14
   (C. 519–465 B.C.)

8. PERICLES    15
   (C.500–429 B.C.)

9. PTOLEMY I    16
   (C. 364–C. 283 B.C.)

10. ALEXANDER THE GREAT    17
    (356–323 B.C.)

11. LIU PANG (KAO-TSU)    18
    (256–195 B.C.)

12. JULIUS CAESAR    19
    (100–44 B.C.)

13. CONSTANTINE THE GREAT    20
    (C. A.D. 280 –337)

14. ALARIC THE GOTH    21
    (C. A.D. 370–410)

15. ATTILA THE HUN    22
    (C. A.D. 406–453)

16. THEODORIC THE GREAT    23
    (C. A.D. 454–526)

17. JUSTINIAN I    24
    (A.D. 482–565)

18. AL-MANSUR    25
    (C. A.D. 714–775)

19. CHARLEMAGNE    26
    (C. A.D. 742–814)

20. ALFRED THE GREAT    27
    (A.D. 848–899)

21. OTTO THE GREAT    28
    (A.D. 912–973)

22. STEPHEN I    29
    (C. A.D. 975–1038)

23. CANUTE THE GREAT    30
    (C. A.D. 995–1035)

24. WILLIAM THE CONQUEROR    31
    (C. 1027–1087)

25. FREDERICK I (BARBAROSSA)    32
    (C. 1123–1190)

26. SALADIN    33
    (1137–1193)

16.
17.
9.
1.   2.   3.   4.   5.  6.7.8. 10. 11. 12.   13. 14.15.   18.
19.

**2500 B.C.**                                    **A.D. 750**

# TABLE OF CONTENTS

**27**. LOTHARIO DE SEGNI
(POPE INNOCENT III)    *34*
(C. 1160–1216)

**28**. PHILIP II (AUGUSTUS)    *35*
(1165–1223)

**29**. GENGHIS KHAN    *36*
(C. 1167–1227)

**30**. JOHN (LACKLAND)    *37*
(1167–1216)

**31**. ROBERT BRUCE    *38*
(1274–1329)

**32**. MARGARET I    *39*
(1353–1412)

**33**. LORENZO DE' MÉDICI
(THE MAGNIFICENT)    *40*
(1449–1492)

**34**. FERDINAND II    *41*
(1452–1516)

**35**. MONTEZUMA II    *42*
(C.1480–1520)

**36**. HENRY VIII    *43*
(1491–1547)

**37**. SULEIMAN I (THE MAGNIFICENT)    *44*
(1494–1566)

**38**. CHARLES V    *45*
(1500–1558)

**39**. PHILIP II    *46*
(1527–1598)

**40**. ELIZABETH I    *47*
(1533–1603)

**41**. LOUIS XIV    *48*
(1638–1715)

**42**. PETER THE GREAT    *49*
(1672–1725)

**43**. FREDERICK THE GREAT    *50*
(1712–1786)

**44**. MARIA THERESA    *51*
(1717–1780)

**45**. CATHERINE THE GREAT    *52*
(1729–1796)

**46**. GEORGE WASHINGTON    *53*
(1732–1799)

**47**. LOUIS XVI    *54*
(1754–1793)

**48**. NAPOLEON BONAPARTE    *55*
(1769–1821)

**49**. SIMÓN BOLÍVAR    *56*
(1783–1830)

**50**. SHAKA    *57*
(C.1787–1828)

**51**. BENJAMIN DISRAELI    *58*
(1804–1881)

**52**. BENITO JUÁREZ    *59*
(1806–1872)

**53**. GIUSEPPE GARIBALDI    *60*
(1807–1882)

28.
29.
20.    21.    22.    23. 24.    25.    26. 27. 30.    31.    32.    33. 34.    35.    39.    42.
36.    38.    40. 41.
37.

A.D. 751                                              1700

# TABLE OF CONTENTS

**54**. ABRAHAM LINCOLN    *61*
(1809–1865)

**55**. OTTO VON BISMARCK    *62*
(1815–1898)

**56**. QUEEN VICTORIA    *63*
(1819–1901)

**57**. PEDRO II    *64*
(1825–1891)

**58**. GEORGES CLÉMENCEAU    *65*
(1841–1929)

**59**. MUTSUHITO (MEIJI)    *66*
(1852–1912)

**60**. WOODROW WILSON    *67*
(1856–1924)

**61**. DAVID LLOYD GEORGE    *68*
(1863–1945)

**62**. ELEUTHERIOS VENIZÉLOS    *69*
(1864–1936)

**63**. SUN YAT-SEN    *70*
(1866–1925)

**64**. NICHOLAS II    *71*
(1868–1918)

**65**. NEVILLE CHAMBERLAIN    *72*
(1869–1940)

**66**. VLADIMIR LENIN    *73*
(1870–1924)

**67**. WINSTON CHURCHILL    *74*
(1874–1965)

**68**. JOSEF STALIN    *75*
(1879–1953)

**69**. MUSTAPHA KEMAL ATATÜRK    *76*
(1881–1938)

**70**. ANGELO RONCALLI (POPE JOHN XXIII) *77*
(1881–1963)

**71**. FRANKLIN D. ROOSEVELT    *78*
(1882–1945)

**72**. BENITO MUSSOLINI    *79*
(1883–1945)

**73**. DAVID BEN-GURION    *80*
(1886–1973)

**74.** CHIANG KAI-SHEK    *81*
(1887–1975)

**75**. ADOLF HITLER    *82*
(1889–1945)

**76**. CHARLES DE GAULLE    *83*
(1890–1970)

**77**. FRANCISCO FRANCO    *84*
(1892–1975)

**78**. HAILE SELASSIE I    *85*
(1892–1975)

**79**. MAO TSE-TUNG    *86*
(1893–1976)

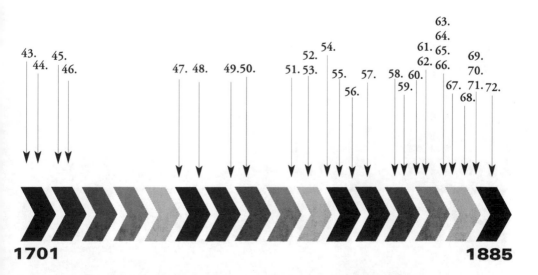

1701                                                                1885

# TABLE OF CONTENTS

**80**. NIKITA KHRUSHCHEV    *87*
(1894–1971)

**81**. JUAN PERÓN    *88*
(1895–1974)

**82**. GOLDA MEIR    *89*
(1898–1978)

**83**. RUHOLLAH  HENDI
(AYATOLLAH KHOMEINI)    *90*
(1900–1989)

**84**. ACHMAD SUKARNO    *91*
(1901–1970)

**85**. HIROHITO    *92*
(1901–1989)

**86**. DAG HAMMARSKJÖLD    *93*
(1905–1961)

**87**. KWAME NKRUMAH    *94*
(1909–1972)

**88**. RONALD REAGAN    *95*
(1911–)

**89**. RICHARD NIXON    *96*
(1913–1994)

**90**. JOHN F. KENNEDY    *97*
(1917–1963)

**91**. INDIRA GANDHI    *98*
(1917–1984)

**92**. FERDINAND MARCOS    *99*
(1917–1989)

**93**. GAMAL ABDEL NASSER    *100*
(1918–1970)

**94**. ANWAR SADAT    *101*
(1918–1981)

**95**. NELSON MANDELA    *102*
(1918– )

**96**. MARGARET THATCHER    *103*
(1925– )

**97**. FIDEL CASTRO    *104*
(1926- )

**98**. MIKHAIL GORBACHEV    *105*
(1931–)

**99**. SADDAM HUSSEIN    *106*
(1937– )

**100**. LECH WALESA    *107*
(1943– )

TRIVIA QUIZ    *108*
INDEX    *109*

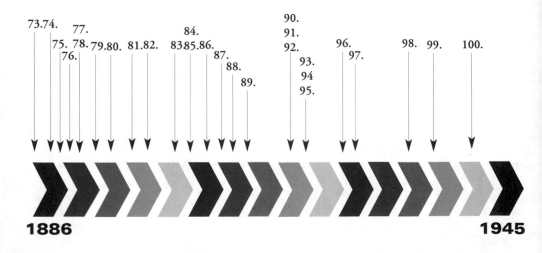

73.74.    77.
75. 78. 79.80.    81.82.    84.    83 85.86.
76.    87.
88.
89.

90.
91.
92.    96.    98. 99. 100.
93.    97.
94
95.

**1886**                                                                **1945**

# INTRODUCTION

Any author attempting to name a definitive list of 100 world leaders who have shaped world history could be said to have a daunting task. After all, from the earliest days of recorded history there have been thousands of people—men and women, young and old, good and evil—who have had a significant impact on the history of the world. Where does one begin? What qualities must a world leader possess? Should a world leader be only someone whose influence stretched beyond the borders of his or her own nation, impacting the world at large? And if so, where does that leave the leaders who made a significant mark in history at a time when the civilized world was a much smaller place than it is today?

In approaching this subject, we have taken a fairly broad view. Our first "world leader" ruled a very small—but very significant—world: the ancient pharaoh, Khufu, who ruled Ancient Egypt, more than 4,5000 years ago. Our final leader is a one-time shipyard electrician who rose from being a labor union activist to the presidency of his small, Eastern European nation: Poland's Solidarity founder, Lech Walesa.

In between these two men, are 98 other men and women who, during their lives, displayed the qualities—both good and bad—that enabled them to leave their imprint on history. Of course, the qualities necessary to be a world leader have changed dramatically over the centuries. For nearly one thousand years, world leaders were men who achieved great power through conquest—often beginning with their own lands, and then spreading their influence by dominating other nations and their peoples. Men such as Alexander the Great, Julius Caesar, Attila the Hun, William the Conqueror, and Genghis Khan would fit into this category. All these leaders combined military, and political skills to dominate their eras—some for only a brief time—and leave their imprint indelibly on the sands of history.

During the Middle Ages, and throughout the Renaissance and the Age of Reason, the rise of powerful monarchs occurred. Such men and women as Philip II (Augustus), Margaret I, Ferdinand II, Henry VIII, Suleiman the Magnificent, Elizabeth I, Louis XIV, Peter the Great, and Catherine the Great ruled vast empires, controlled great wealth, and created lasting monuments to their rule by building great cities, developing classic architecture, and instituting many cultural advancements that influence our world even today.

Over the past two hundred years, the "profiles" of world leaders have changed again. No longer conquerors or monarchs, the men and women who later stepped onto history's center stage were liberators, revolutionaries, diplomats—and as democracies began to form throughout the world—elected heads of state. Leaders as diverse as Benito Juárez, Giuseppe Garibaldi, Benjamin Disraeli, Woodrow Wilson, Winston Churchill, Franklin D. Roosevelt, Mao-Tse-tung, Golda Meir, and Nelson Mandela helped free and unify their people by throwing off the yoke of colonialism, or guided their nations through crises such as wars and economic depressions, in the process proving worthy of the status of a world leader.

In addition to these people, this book contains biographies of other notable figures, some of whom are harder to categorize, but whose impact on history in undeniable: Siddhartha Gautama (The Buddha), Lorenzo de Médici (the Magnificent), Napoleon Bonaparte, Adolf Hitler, Pope John XXIII, Dag Hammarskjöld, and Hirohito.

Ultimately, the 100 world leaders we have chosen perhaps share at least one common attribute—an inner fortitude that enabled them to rise to greatness, even though some of them took the path away from accomplishing great things, and wound up destroying themselves and everything they had built. We believe that each person whose biography is contained in this book is a fascinating subject for historical study—and we hope you think so, too.

# 1. Khufu
## (c.2500 B.C.)

The second king of the Fourth dynasty of Egypt's Old Kingdom, the pharaoh **Khufu** is best remembered for building the **Great Pyramid** at Giza to serve as a tomb upon his death.

Historians do not know very much about Khufu because very few written records remain from this period. What is known is that Khufu was the son and successor of King Snefru and his queen Hetepheres. Khufu ruled a unified Egypt and many of his relatives assisted him in governing. He was probably married four times: to Merityetes, who was buried in one of the three small pyramids beside his own; to a second unknown queen; to Henutsen, whose small pyramid is the third of the group; and to Nefert-kau, the eldest of Snefru's daughters and Khufu's sister.

For years the history of Khufu's dynasty was known through the writings of the Greek historian **Herodotus**, who described the reign as one of oppression and misery. Khufu's later reputation in Egypt as a wise ruler, however, contradicts these writings.

Khufu's legacy is for building ancient Egypt's most famous lasting monument, the Great Pyramid at Giza. To create this 5,750,000-ton edifice, a masterpiece of technical skill and engineering, approximately 2.3 million blocks of stone were cut, transported, and assembled. It took thousands of workers 20 years to complete the Great Pyramid, which rose to a height of 481 feet at a base of 13 acres, and was built at the center of a huge complex of temples, statues, monuments, and lesser tombs of the pharaoh's family.

Herodotus asserts that the cruel tyrant Khufu used slave labor who toiled in the hot sun to build the pyramid. Later historians suggest that the construction was a public works project, which kept the rather well-treated agricultural laborers busy and fed when the Nile River was flooding, and there was little work to do in the fields.

By the late 20th century, archaeologists found evidence that a more limited work force may have occupied the site permanently rather than on a seasonal basis. The excavated laborers' districts included bakeries, storage areas, workshops, and the small tombs of workers and artisans.

Scholars are not even quite sure how the Great Pyramid was built. One theory holds that builders used a long ramp stretching out into the desert, and this ramp was continually lengthened and heightened as the pyramid grew higher. Another possible method involved using a circular ramp that rose and wound around the pyramid's exterior as it followed each layer of blocks upward.

Khufu ruled Egypt for more than 20 years, and after he died, two of his sons, Djedefre and Khafre, succeeded him.

**Building of the Great Pyramid at Giza**

# Sargon the Great
## (c.2300 B.C.)

**Sargon the Great** was a Semitic king who built the world's the first real empire in **Mesopotamia**, unifying Sumerian territory with the capital he founded at Akkad.

Much of the historical record concerning Sargon comes from fragmentary sources and legend. Historians believe he grew up in humble circumstances; one story says that a gardener found the infant Sargon floating in a basket on the river and brought him up in his own calling. Sargon's father is unknown, and his mother is said to have been a priestess in a town on the middle of the Euphrates River. Sargon rose to power, therefore, without the help of influential relatives.

Sargon came from Kish and had a high position in service of the court of its ruler, Urzababa. After a military failure by Urzababa, and some confusion about succession, Sargon seized power and built a new capital at Akkad. At the beginning of Sargon's reign, **Lugalzaggesi** of Uruk (in present-day Iraq) had already united the independent city-states of Sumer by defeating each in turn; Lugalzaggesi claimed to rule not only the lands of the Sumerian city-states, but also those as far west as the Mediterranean, and he had established trade contracts from the Indus Valley to as far away as Crete.

Sargon first defeated Lugalzaggesi at Uruk, and then in a series of battles, conquered the last of the independent states of Sumer. Subsequently, the charismatic and powerful Akkadian ruler gained control of the Persian Gulf, conquered Elam, the mountain lands of present-day Iran, Upper Mesopotamia, and present-day Syria. Thus his empire stretched from the **Persian Gulf** to the **Mediterranean Sea**. Some later legends claimed that he even extended his conquests into Anatolia (present-day Turkey) and across the sea to Crete.

As a result of Sargon's military prowess and his ability to organize a highly centralized government, as well as the existing commercial ties between the old Sumerian city-states he conquered and other regions, the Akkadian ruler enriched his kingdom with trade. Goods were exchanged with the peoples of the Indus Valley, the coast of Oman, the islands and shores of the Persian Gulf, Badakhshan (near the present-day border of Afghanistan and China), the Taurus Mountains, Cappadocia, Crete, and perhaps even Greece.

Rebellions—probably caused by the inability of one man, however energetic, to control so vast an empire—troubled the latter part of Sargon's reign. Two of his sons, Rimush and Manishtushu, succeeded him and helped further consolidate the empire.

**Sargon**

# 3. Hammurabi
## (c.1792–c.1750 B.C.)

**Hammurabi**, king of Babylon, is best remembered for developing the world's first written legal code, a series of laws that governed all aspects of life for the **Babylonian Empire**.

Hammurabi was a well-known and respected monarch remembered for bringing "order and righteousness in the land." However, his code was little more than forgotten folklore until 1902 when French archaeologists excavating in present-day southwestern Iran discovered a seven-foot high stone slab with the Legal Code of Hammurabi carved in cuneiform.

**Hammurabi's Code** depicts him as shepherd of his people and a just ruler. The Code covered civil, criminal, and commercial matters. The 282 laws specified conduct—and where necessary, punishments—in everything ranging from murder to the illegal felling of trees. Penalties for breaking the laws could be

**Hammurabi**

severe and were based, for the most part, on the principle of the *Lex Talionis*—the punishment fits the crime. Therefore, the Code said that: "If a man has put out the eye of another man, they shall put out this eye." Punishments were meted out according to social status, with some violations compensated by silver.

Since the king was also the empire's chief priest, the Code also governed Babylonian religious life. For the first time, laws were published and codified for all to see, and in this manner Hammurabi's Code was the precursor of the legal systems under which most modern societies still function.

During his reign, Hammurabi brought Babylon to preeminence in the Mesopotamian world, where it remained for more than a thousand years. Along with his legal system, he installed a centralized government and formed a standing army. When he came to power, his kingdom was 80 miles long and 20 miles wide, surrounded by much larger states and more powerful rulers. After spending seven years to strengthen his realm from within, Hammurabi ventured to expand his borders. In time, his kingdom stretched as far as the Persian Gulf and to parts of Assyria. Through expansion, he not only added new territory, but also acquired needed raw materials.

Hammurabi also engaged in the traditional activities of an ancient Mesopotamian king: building and restoring temples, city walls, and public buildings, digging canals, and dedicating cult objects to the deities in the cities and towns of his realm. His letters show that he personally engaged in the details of implementing these changes.

The last few years of Hammurabi's reign were without major conflicts, but by this time, he was a sick man. When he died around 1750 B.C., his son, Samsuiluna, was already carrying the burden of governing the empire.

# 4. King David
## (c. 1010–c. 970 B.C.)

The second and greatest king of the Israelites, **David** united Israel and Judah, and established a strong kingdom with Jerusalem as its capital.

The youngest son of Jesse of Bethlehem—and grandson of Boaz and Ruth—David spent his youth tending sheep; he then entered King **Saul's** service as a harpist. At the time, the Israelite's most deadly enemy was the **Philistines**, a prosperous and technologically advanced people, who ruled the Palestinian interior. David became Saul's principal commander and won several military campaigns. He formed a close friendship with Saul's son and heir, Jonathan, and married Saul's daughter Michal.

**King David**

After David's many successful forays against the Philistines, Saul became jealous and sought to assassinate the young man. However, David formed an army with Israelites dissatisfied with Saul, who soon lost his own life at the hands of the Philistines on Mount Gilboa. His son Jonathan was also slain.

Over the years David had gained the favor of many Judean elders by protecting them against their enemies; thus he was elected king of Judah, not as a rebel against Saul, but as his true successor. He soon gained power over the northern tribes, and eventually took over the rule of Israel. To control both lands, David and his army conquered **Jerusalem**, along a route linking the two kingdoms, and he made the city his capital. He went on to conquer the Philistines and made them a vassal state.

In Israel's religious tradition, the king mediated between the deity and his people, and was thought of as both human and divine. In Jerusalem, David based his rule on the ancient cult of Mt. Zion, renaming it the cult of **Yahweh**, by whose power he had conquered. David then brought the **Ark of the Covenant** to Jerusalem, making it the center of the cult. This rectangular wooden box, represented the presence of Yahweh amidst the people of Israel. Thus, David was both military and spiritual leader of his people.

David had many wives and concubines, and many of his children caused troubles. His son Absalom, by his wife Haggith, rose up against his father after David's eldest son raped Absalom's sister and David did not retaliate. David left the city, returned with his mercenaries, and Absalom was overcome. David also put down a second rebellion, led by Sheba, another of his sons. Throughout the remainder of his rule, David faced recurrent wars with the Philistines, but he never suffered a major defeat. When he died, his kingdom stretched from the Euphrates River in the northeast to the Gulf of Aqaba in the southeast.

Upon David's death, his son Solomon, by his wife Bathsheba, succeeded him.

# 5. Cyrus the Great
## (c. 600–530 B.C.)

Founder of the one of the world's earliest and greatest empires, **Cyrus the Great** came to power by defeating his own grandfather, Astyages, king of Media and overlord of the **Persians**.

**Cyrus**

According to legend, Astyages gave his daughter in marriage to a Persian prince named Cambyses. From their union, Cyrus was born. Meanwhile, Astyages had a dream that the baby would grow up to overthrow him and ordered Cyrus to be killed. Instead, Astyages's chief advisor gave the baby to a shepherd to raise.

When the outstanding qualities of the 10-year old Cyrus came to the attention of Astyages, the king was persuaded to let the boy live. After Cyrus reached manhood he gathered the forces of other Persian tribes and revolted against his grandfather. Mindful of the dream, Astyages marched against the rebel, but his army deserted him and he sur-

rendered to Cyrus in 550 B.C. Cyrus then entered the Median capital of Ecbatana (present-day Hamadan) and took the throne as king of a Persian Empire.

Two years later, Cyrus went to war against **Croesus**, the king of Lydia (present-day Turkey); the Persian ruler captured Croesus and took the fabulous wealth of his kingdom for himself. Then Cyrus turned his attention to **Babylon**. Nabonidus, the Babylonian ruler, was an unpopular king. He paid too little attention to the affairs of his kingdom, and had alienated the native Babylonian priesthood. Cyrus took advantage of this fact, and the greatest city in the Middle East fell swiftly. In the late summer of 539 B.C., Cyrus marched into Babylon and seized the hands of the statue of the **Marduk**, the god of the city, as a signal of his desire to rule as a Babylonian and not as a foreign conqueror. Many of the Babylonians hailed him as the legitimate successor to the throne.

Cyrus's policies toward his subjects were enlightened and tolerant. The Medians had access to important administrative posts, and the Hebrews were freed from their Babylonian captivity and allowed to start rebuilding the Temple at Jerusalem. Generally Cyrus refrained from interfering with the native customs and religions of the different peoples under his reign.

After the capture of Babylon, Cyrus came to control a vast empire, stretching from the Indus River to the Mediterranean, from the Caucasus to the Indian Ocean. Through his conquests, the richness of Persian culture was spread to much of the then-developed world.

In 530 B.C., Cyrus tried to repel attacks on the northern section of his empire by the nomadic Massagetai tribes. However, his troops were defeated and he was killed. Cyrus was buried at Pasaegadae (in modern-day Iran). His son Cambyses II succeeded him.

# 6. Siddhartha Gautama (The Buddha)
## (c.563–483 B.C)

The founder of **Buddhism**, **Siddhartha Gautama** is one of the most significant leaders in the history of the world's religions. For more than two thousand years, Buddhism has played a central role in the spiritual, cultural, and social life of millions of people around the world.

Born around 563 B.C., the son of a local ruler in northern India, Siddhartha was raised in the luxury of his father's realm. At age 16, he married a neighboring princess, and they became the parents of at least one child. As he grew older, Siddhartha continued to be shielded from life's problems. Four times he left the palace for brief periods; each time he encountered pain. He saw an old man, a sick man, a dead man, and a man committed to the religious life. These encounters with life's hardships are known to Buddhists today as the **Four Meetings**. They changed Siddhartha's life; from that point on, he sought an answer to the universal problem of pain.

Despite his comfortable existence, Siddhartha became discontented. At the age of 29, against his family's wishes, he left the palace, renounced his privileged existence, and began a spiritual quest that lasted for six years. He placed himself under the spiritual guidance of two recluses, following their meditative discipline. Disappointed with their methods, he left them and joined the Jains, an austere group that did not believe in harming any living thing. However, after five years of practicing Jainism, Siddhartha realized that he still hadn't found the answers he longed for.

At around the age of 35, Siddhartha journeyed to Bodh-Gaya in northeast India. He rested under a fig tree, letting his mind wander over his previous experiences. After his long meditation, Siddhartha had a spiritual awakening, a full "enlightenment." He began to teach what he had learned, and soon many followers flocked to him. As his teachings spread, he became known as the Buddha, the Enlightened One.

Buddha taught the **Four Noble Truths**. First, all existence is suffering; there is no escape from the pain of human existence. Second, the cause for the suffering comes from desire; third, the release from suffering comes when desire ceases. Fourth, the way to cease the suffering is through the **Eight-Fold Path**.

**A giant bronze statue of the Buddah**

The Eight-Fold path consists of: right understanding, right thoughts, right speech, right action, right livelihood, right effort, right mindfulness, and right mediation. By following this correct path—dharma—the soul can achieve a state of **Nirvana**, a perfect final state of peace.

For the next 45 years, the Buddha taught his beliefs to many followers. Through his teachings, and those of his many disciples, Buddhism became one of the world's major religions.

# 7. Xerxes I
## (c.519–465 B.C. )

Great-grandson of Cyrus the Great (see no. 5), the founder of the Persian Empire, **Xerxes I** tried to complete a job left unfinished by his father, Darius I—the conquest of **Greece**.

Before Darius died in 486 B.C., he had succeeded in expanding the empire by consolidating Persian rule over Egypt. However, his eventual goal of conquering the Greek city-states was thwarted when the outnumbered, but better-trained Greeks, defeated him at the Battle of Marathon in 490 B.C.

Ten years later, Xerxes set about accomplishing what his father had been unable to do. First, Xerxes suppressed a revolt in Egypt, where a usurper had

**Xerxes I**

been governing for two years. Xerxes left one of his brothers, Achaemenes, in charge of the Egyptians, who now had to pay new taxes and endure the confiscation of materials from their temples.

A major revolt in Babylonia about 482 B.C. temporarily halted Xerxes' plans to finish the invasion into Greece. As in Egypt, Xerxes suppressed this uprising with a heavy hand, destroying the great ziggurat (pyramidal temple) and the temple of Marduk.

Finally in 481 B.C., Xerxes turned his attention to Greece. He led a combined land and sea invasion, with estimated forces of 300,000 men. The invaders took northern Greece in the summer of 480 B.C., and proceeded south, toward the narrow mountain pass at **Thermopylae**. There some 300

Spartan warriors fought a valiant battle, delaying the Persian advance and inflicting heavy loses on the invaders before they finally broke through. The Persian land forces then marched on Athens, taking the city and burning the Acropolis.

On the sea, while the Persians had lost many ships because of stormy weather, they still had a more than two-to-one advantage when they met the Greeks in the narrow straits of **Salamis**. Still, the Greeks emerged victorious, using a strategy of setting fire to many Persian vessels, and outmaneuvering the rest in the narrow waters they knew so well.

Xerxes withdrew from Athens and Greece and returned home; he regrouped over the winter and returned the following spring to meet the Greeks on the **Plain of Plataea**. Once again the outnumbered Greeks defeated the larger and more powerful Persian forces, bringing to an end any hopes Xerxes had of conquering Greece.

Although Xerxes never succeeded in his conquest of Greece, the Persian Empire reached its height under his reign; thereafter, it began to decline. In 465 B.C., Xerxes was assassinated in a palace plot by the captain of the bodyguard, **Atabaus**, who planned to take over the throne. Atabaus deceived one of Xerxes' sons, Artaxerxes, into thinking his brother Darius had killed their father. When Artaxerxes found out the truth, he killed Atabaus and ascended the throne.

# 8. Pericles
## (c. 500–429 B.C. )

Politician, statesman, and military leader, **Pericles** dominated the political and intellectual life of democratic **Athens** when that city-state was at the height of its imperial power and cultural greatness.

Born around 500 B.C., Pericles was a descendant of a wealthy family, and enjoyed a progressive education. He entered politics around 469 B.C. A great orator, he became a leader in the Athenian democracy movement, and rose to become the most powerful ruler in Athens. Under his leadership Athens reached its greatest political and cultural heights.

Pericles was a patron of the arts, and during this period Athenian architecture and sculpture reached their greatest development. Numerous public buildings were constructed, including such marvels as the **Parthenon**; literature and fine art flourished as never before; and dramatic festivals were held, which even the poorer citizens could attend. Athens became the most magnificent city of the ancient world.

Under Pericles Athens also became a strong military power. He built the Athenian fleet into one of the greatest in the world, and he led its army in many battles, attacking Delphi and putting down revolts in Euboea and Samos. Politically he introduced a truly democratic system in which anyone cold hold public office. He also initiated salaries for civil servants and allowances for the poor.

Around 450 B.C., Pericles met a woman named **Aspasia**, who had come to Athens and opened a school of rhetoric and philosophy. Many of the daughters and wives of Athens' leaders studied with her, and she soon became widely known. Pericles fell in love with Aspasia; he divorced his wife, and although he was forbidden to marry Aspasia because she was a foreigner, they made a home and life together.

Despite his many successes, Pericles was unable to put an end to the many wars that had plagued Athens and the other Greek city-states. In 431 B.C., the rival city-state, **Sparta**, broke a peace treaty and declared war on Athens. This action set off three decades of conflict known as the **Peloponnesian War**.

The war began well for Athens and Pericles was hailed for his military strategy. When the Spartans invaded, Pericles persuaded the Athenians to abandon the countryside, retreat within the city's walls, and to rely on their fleet. Then, in the war's second year, a plague struck, ravaging the city. Pericles was attacked by his enemies, and was briefly deposed from the leadership. He was soon reelected with more powers; however, shortly after that, the plague claimed Pericles as one of its victims.

After his death, the Athenian state gradually declined, caused by the continuing war with Sparta, and the failure to find a replacement for the dynamic leadership of Pericles.

**Pericles**

**Ptolemy**, a Macedonian general who fought alongside **Alexander the Great**, became the ruler of **Egypt** and the founder of the Ptolemaic dynasty, which reigned for nearly three centuries.

Ptolemy was the son of the nobleman Lagus and Arsinoe, who was related to the Macedonian Argead dynasty and had formerly been a concubine of Alexander's father, Philip II. As a youth, Ptolemy served as a page at the Macedonian royal court, where he became closely associated with the young crown prince, Alexander. After Alexander's accession to the throne in 336 B.C., Ptolemy joined the king's bodyguard.

Before long, Ptolemy had become one of Alexander's most trusted generals, playing a major role in Alexander's campaigns in Afghanistan and India around 327-326 B.C. The young king decorated Ptolemy several times for his deeds, and married him to the Persian Aracama at a mass wedding at Susa. The wedding sealed Alexander's policy of merging the Macedonian and Persian populations. Artacama was only one of Ptolemy's four wives.

After Alexander's death in 323 B.C., his vast empire was divided up among several of his generals. Ptolemy became satrap (governor) of Egypt. During his reign, the administrative, financial, and commercial infrastructures developed. He established a glorious new capital at Alexandria, which would become the greatest city in the world. Its museum and grand library attracted scholars from many countries. Besides being a patron of the arts and sciences, Ptolemy was a writer himself. In the last few years of his life, he wrote a generally reliable history of Alexander the Great's campaigns.

Throughout his lengthy reign, Ptolemy waged many wars against foreign rulers in an effort to both solidify his hold on Egypt and expand his territory. Despite these wars, Ptolemy governed well, and under his rule Egypt became a formidable power. By the time of his death, he controlled Cyprus, Palestine, and many cities in the **Aegean** and **Asia Minor**. During the last 15 years of his reign, Ptolemy turned to securing and expanding his empire through a policy of alliances and marriages rather than through warfare.

As he neared the end of his life, Ptolemy made provisions for a successor. In 290 B.C. his wife, Berenice, became queen of Egypt, and in 285 B.C. his younger son Ptolemy II Philadelphus, who was born in 308 B.C., became co-regent and successor. The provision for the succession made possible a peaceful transition when Ptolemy died in the winter of 283 B.C. After his death, the Egyptians proclaimed him a god.

The last of the Ptolemaic rulers was Queen Cleopatra VII, paramour of Julius Caesar and Marc Anthony.

**Ptolemy II meeting with his architects**

# 10. Alexander the Great
## (356–323 B.C.)

The greatest conqueror of the ancient world, **Alexander the Great** ruled a vast empire that straddled both Europe and Asia, and spread the Greek language and culture over much of the known world.

This remarkable leader was born at Pella in **Macedonia**, the son of King Philip II and Olympias, daughter of the king of Epirus. The Greek philosopher Aristotle tutored Alexander from the ages of 13 to 16; Alexander showed a keen mind, and his teacher inspired him to an interest in philosophy, medicine, and science.

Alexander's parents divorced, and his future became uncertain after he sided with his mother in a dispute with his father; he was forced to flee with her to Epirus. Shortly afterward, though, father and son were reconciled and Alexander returned. When Philip was assassinated in 336 B.C., the army proclaimed Alexander as successor, and he assumed the kingship.

After taking retribution against those he believed were responsible for his father's murder, Alexander marched southward and brought a wavering Thessaly under control. When a false rumor of his death precipitated a revolt of Theban democrats, Alexander demanded their surrender. When they refused, he entered Thebes, and razed it to the ground, sparing only temples and the poet Pindar's house. Alexander's army slaughtered 6,000 Thebans, and sold the survivors into slavery.

**Alexander the Great**

One major goal Alexander had was to continue his father's campaign to punish the **Persians** for Xerxes's invasion of Greece nearly 150 years earlier. In 333 B.C., Alexander fought a major battle against **Darius III**, king of the Persians, at Issus (in modern-day Turkey). Alexander used the mobility of his troops to confuse and defeat the much larger Persian army.

Alexander then marched into **Egypt** where the people welcomed him without resistance, and the high priests acclaimed him as a god. In 331 B.C., in a final attempt to destroy Darius and his entire army, Alexander won a second great battle against the much larger Persian army at Arabela. Darius escaped, but was later killed by one of his own generals. The victorious Alexander marched into the Persian capital, Persepolis, and razed it. He thereafter ruled the Persian Empire in cooperation with the Persian nobles, some of whom he appointed as his governors. Alexander spent the next several years trying to spread Greek culture to all reaches of his growing empire; he wanted to merge the Greeks, Persians, and Macedonians together into one ethnic group.

Alexander marched his army all the way to the Indus River, where he fought a battle against Indian troops and their elephants. Finally, in 326 B.C., his weary forces demanded to return home. On the journey back, Alexander died in Babylon in 323 B.C. He was buried in **Alexandria**, Egypt, a city he had founded.

# 11. Liu Pang (Kao-tsu)
## (256–195 B.C.)

**Liu Pang** was the founder and first emperor of the **Han** dynasty, which lasted 400 years, and under which the Chinese imperial system assumed most of the characteristics it would keep until the 20th century.

Born to a peasant family, Liu Pang was a police officer under the Ch'in dynasty. In 210 B.C., after the death of the Ch'in emperor Shih Huang-ti, who had been the first to unify China, Liu joined the rebels under the leadership of **Hsiang Yü**. Hsiang was a warlord who tried to restore the feudal system, reinstating many of the former nobles and dividing the land among his generals. Since Liu Pang was an important leader, he received control of the kingdom of Han in West China (present-day Szechwan and southern Shensi provinces).

By 206 B.C., Hsiang and Liu turned against each other; Liu's peasant shrewdness helped lead him to victory over his militarily brilliant, but politically naive, rival. The civil war ended in 202 B.C., when Hsiang Yü took his own life, rather than surrender. Liu then became ruler of China, taking the name of Han Kao-tsu, or "Exulted Emperor of Han." He then began the lengthy process of reunifying China.

In domestic affairs, Liu instituted a system of laissez-faire politics. The rulers in the populous eastern part of the empire were sons of the emperor and *marquisates*, local aristocratic supporters of the throne who collected taxes in return for land.

In the western half, 14 commanderies ruled. These officials, rather than the emperor, initiated most policy proposals, which Kao-tsu then discussed among his ministerial advisors before reaching a decision.

Kao-tsu was a coarse man who disdained education. Nevertheless, he was both pragmatic and flexible, recognizing the need for the presence of educated men at court. He showed particular concern for reviving the rural economy and for lightening the tax burden of the peasants and their conscription as laborers. His policies led to population growth, expansion of the economy, and a flourishing culture.

In foreign affairs, Kao-tsu used a skillful combination of diplomacy and force. To gain the support of otherwise belligerent nomad chieftains, he offered gifts, particularly that of silk and the hand of a Han daughter in marriage.

Although Kao-tsu intensely disliked the teachings of the once popular **Confucius** (551–479 B.C.) and philosophers in general, his successors would incorporate Confucianism into their governments as they continued the process of consolidating and expanding the empire. While Kao-tsu's rule was short, it nevertheless set the stage for the Han dynasty to flower; subsequent Han rulers would establish the **Mandarin** social and political system, which survived as the basis of Chinese society right up until the mid-20th century and the advent of Communism.

**Rider from Han dynasty**

A brilliant military leader and the first sole ruler of the **Roman Empire**, **Julius Caesar** expanded the power and glory of Rome before being destroyed by the betrayal of his former supporters.

Gaius Julius Caesar was born into a patrician family. After joining the Roman army and serving in Asia, Caesar returned to Rome, entered politics and rose quickly to powerful positions. He became *Pontifex Maximus* (high priest) in 63 B.C. as part of a deal with the general **Pompey** (Caesar's son-in-law), and **Crassus**, a banker; together they formed the so-called first triumvirate, a ruling group of three.

In 59 B.C., Caesar became governor of southern Gaul (present-day France); he soon set out on a military campaign to enhance his own power and extend the glory of Rome. He subjugated the rest of Gaul, conquered Helvetii (present-day Switzerland), Belgica (present-day Belgium), crossed the River Rhine to fight the German tribes, and made two expeditions to Britain.

Caesar's brilliance as a commander inspired great loyalty among his soldiers. His acumen as a general alarmed the Roman aristocrats, who feared he might take control of Rome. The Senate, induced by Pompey—by now his enemy and rival—ordered him back to Rome, but without his army. Caesar defied the order; leading his army, he crossed the **Rubicon**, a small river that separated his province in Gaul from Italy, and civil war ensued.

Caesar took Rome, and then pursued the fleeing Pompey to Greece, where Caesar defeated him at the **Battle of Pharsalus**, in 48 B.C. Caesar then campaigned in Asia Minor, Egypt, Africa, and Spain, before returning to Rome in 45 B.C.

After Caesar's conquest in Rome, the Senate had appointed him as director for a term of ten years; he governed Rome as dictator from 49 B.C., as "perpetual" dictator in 44 B.C. His wide-ranging program of reform included the institution of the Julian calendar, the lowering of taxes, the extension of citizenship to more provincials, and initiating a public works program to provide employment and also beautify the city.

**Julius Caesar**

However, Caesar flaunted his ascendancy and ignored Rome's republican traditions. Some of his enemies alleged that he wanted to be king, which was anathema to Romans. A politician named **Cassius** conspired with a former colleague and friend of Caesar's named **Marcus Brutus** to assassinate the leader. As Caesar entered the Roman Senate on the 15th of March 44 B.C., he was stabbed to death.

Caesar's murder plunged Rome into yet another civil war; eventually Caesar's chosen successor, his great-nephew **Gaius Octavius**, defeated his rivals to become the first emperor of the Roman Empire. Julius Caesar was later deified, and a temple was dedicated to his worship in the Forum.

# 13. Constantine the Great
## (c. A.D. 280–337)

As emperor of the Roman Empire, **Constantine** changed the course of history by ending centuries of Christian persecution and making **Christianity** the empire's official religion.

Constantine was the son of a Roman army officer, Constantius, and Helena of Bithynia, his wife or concubine for 19 years. By the early 4th century, the Roman Empire had become divided; one ruler led the Western Empire (Italy, Gaul, Britain, and Spain), while another controlled the Eastern Empire (Greece, Syria, Asia Minor and Egypt). In A.D. 305, Constantius became the emperor of the **Western Empire**. When he died the next year, the army proclaimed Constantine the new emperor.

However, a period of unrest ensued, with several persons competing for power; Constantine had to wage several battles to retain control. By A.D. 312 he had defeated all his rivals, with the exception of his brother-in-law, **Maxentius**. Just before the crucial battle with Maxentius at the Milvian Bridge near Rome, Constantine supposedly saw a vision in the sky with the sign of the cross as a battle standard. When he killed Maxentius and won the battle, Constantine took it as a sign of approval. After his victory, he declared himself a Christian.

In A.D. 313, Constantine had a meeting with **Licinius**, emperor of the Eastern Empire. Out of the meeting came Constantine's proclamation, the **Edict of Milan**, which gave equal rights to people of all religions and ended the persecutions of Christians.

Constantine and Licinius fought in A.D. 314, over mutually owned territories. The victorious Constantine was ceded Illyricum (on the east Adriatic coast), Pannonia (the area around present-day Hungary), and Greece, and peace was restored. However, in A.D. 323, serious problems arose again. Constantine won a major battle at Adrianople (present-day Greece), and emerged as the sole ruler of the full empire.

Constantine reunited the empire under his rule. He reorganized the army, recruiting more cavalry troops and creating a more mobile force, which enabled the empire to better defend itself against its enemies.

Constantine also created a new imperial capital at **Constantinople** (present-day Istanbul). It was chosen because of its strategic proximity to the Danube and Euphrates frontiers, and the economic importance of the harbor.

As a committed Christian, Constantine wanted to settle a major internal dispute over doctrine between the eastern and western factions of the church. In A.D. 325, he convened the Council of Nicaea, a conference of 220 bishops representing both sides. The meeting resulted in the **Nicaea Creed**, which set out the basic Christian beliefs upon which both sides could agree. Constantine then established Christianity as the state religion throughout the Roman Empire.

Constantine was baptized a Christian a few weeks before he died in May A.D. 337 His burial site immediately became a place of pilgrimage.

**Constantine**

# 14. Alaric the Goth
## (c. A.D. 370–410)

As warlord and leader of the **Visigoths, Alaric** led the army that sacked Rome in A.D. 410, an event that symbolized the fall of the Western Roman Empire.

Alaric was born on the island of Peuce, at the mouth of the Danube River in present-day Romania. A nobleman by birth, he commanded the Gothic (Germanic) troops in the Roman army, and helped defeat the Western usurper Emperor Eugenius in A.D. 394. Shortly after the death of Emperor Theodosius I the following year, Alaric left the army and the Visigoth tribe elected him as their chief.

In 390 A.D., complaining that his tribe had not been given promised subsidies, Alaric marched his forces against the Eastern Roman Empire, centered at Constantinople. His advance was halted by Roman forces under the command of **Flavius Stilicho**.

In A.D. 395 Alaric moved southward into Greece, where he sacked Piraeus, and ravaged the cities of Corinth, Megara, Argos, and Sparta. The Eastern Emperor Arcadius finally placated the Visigoths in A.D. 397 with a bribe. He then appointed Alaric governor of **Illyricum**.

In A.D. 401, Alaric turned his attention to the Western Empire and invaded Italy, but once again he was thwarted by Stilicho; Roman troops defeated Alaric in A.D. 402, at Pollentia and forced the Visigoths to withdraw from the Italian peninsula. Alaric invaded a second time, and his efforts once more met with defeat. At this time, he entered into a peace treaty with Stilicho. Despite his losses, Alaric eventually convinced the Senate at Rome to pay a large subsidy to his tribe.

After Emperor **Honorius** had Stilicho executed in August A.D. 408, Alaric asked the emperor for land and supplies, a request he refused. The Visigothic chieftain then laid siege to Rome until the Senate agreed to another subsidy and assistance in his negotiations with Honorius. The emperor remained intransigent, however, and in A.D. 409 Alaric again surrounded Rome; he lifted his blockade only after proclaiming his own man, Attalus, as emperor. Attalus then appointed Alaric commander-in-chief of the Roman forces.

**Alaric in Athens**

After Alaric deposed Attalus in the summer of A.D. 410, the Visigoths besieged Rome for the third time. When Alaric's allies within Rome opened the gates to him, his troops occupied the city, which had not been captured by a foreign enemy for nearly 800 years. The Visigoths plundered the city, ravaging the buildings and monuments for three days.

Alaric then tried to follow through with his plan to occupy Sicily and Africa, but on the way to those lands, a storm destroyed his fleet. He died suddenly just a few months after the assault on Rome. Legend says that he was buried at a secret location on the Busento River.

A ruthless but natural leader of fighting men, **Attila** led his warriors in a series of bloody campaigns that nearly destroyed the foundation of Western Christendom.

The Huns were a warlike nomadic people from **Central Asia** who swept into the Black Sea and Danube River regions around A.D. 370. Their arrival displaced many of the Visigothic and Ostrogothic tribespeople who posed less of a threat to the Romans than did the Huns.

In A.D. 433, Attila and his brother Bleda inherited the leadership of the tribe from their uncle. The brothers jointly ruled a chiefdom that stretched from the Alps and the Baltic in the west to somewhere near the Caspian Sea in the east. At the time, the Huns were receiving an annual tribute of 700 pounds of gold from the Eastern Roman Empire in Constantinople as a price for peace.

While the Vandals in northern Africa were threatening Egypt—the granary for the Middle East—and also the supply lines to Constantinople, Attila took advantage of the situation. He ignored the truce between the Huns and the Eastern Empire, and moved against Roman forts on the north bank of the Danube in A.D. 440. He attacked and destroyed towns and cities as far south as present-day Sofia, Bulgaria. Attila's invasion won concessions from the emperor; the annual tribute was raised to 2,100 pounds of gold.

Around A.D. 445, Attila murdered his brother Bleda, and became ruler of the Huns.

In A.D. 451, this "Scourge of God" decided to attack the **Western Roman Empire**, invading Gaul with an enormous army composed of Huns, and various other tribespeople. At the **Battle of Chalons** Attila met his only defeat, at the hands of combined Roman, Frankish, and Visigoths forces. While the Visigoth king Theodoric was killed in the fierce fighting, the Huns and their allies suffered heavy losses.

After withdrawing from Gaul, Attila then turned on Italy, where his forces destroyed several northern towns and occupied Milan. With his army set to march on Rome, Pope **Leo I** came north and met with Attila, who had high regard for men and women with spiritual qualities. After their conversation, Attila decided to leave Italy. Pope Leo I became the champion of Christianity, although some historians believe that with famine and pestilence raging in Italy, the Huns would have been compelled to leave anyway.

In A.D. 453, as he recrossed the Alps, Attila died during the evening of his marriage to a young Hunnite woman. A legend says that after a heavy feast and excessive drinking, he suffered a bloody nose and drowned in his own blood.

Shortly after his death, the Huns broke into smaller groups and their influence declined.

**Attila the Hun**

# 16. Theodoric the Great
## (c. A.D. 454–526)

The reign of **Theodoric**, king of the **Ostrogroths** and founder of the Ostrogothic Kingdom in Italy, brought about the beginnings of the synthesis of Roman and German cultures.

Theodoric was born in the Roman province of Pannonia (present-day Hungary). Sent as a hostage to Constantinople at the age of eight, he was educated there in Greco-Roman cultural values and remained until he was seventeen. Elected king in A.D. 471 after his father's death, Theodoric became involved in intrigues both against and with the Byzantine Emperor Zeno, who in the late A.D. 480s finally sent him on conquest to Italy to be rid of him.

In A.D. 493, after a three-year siege of **Ravenna**, Theodoric forced the surrender of Odoacer, the German leader who had deposed the last Roman emperor, Romulus Augustulus. Theodoric had Odoacer killed, and then became ruler of Italy, with Ravenna as his capital. Such an invasion promised a homeland for Theodoric's wandering people. At its greatest size, his empire included Italy, Sicily, Dalmatia, and parts of Germany.

Though the Romans and the Germanic peoples differed in creed, race, and culture, Theodoric managed to hold together his kingdom during his 33-year reign. He maintained law and order, preserved Roman legal institutions, and appointed Roman officials to civil service jobs, while retaining a Gothic army. He zealously encouraged trade and skilled crafts. Improvements were made in agriculture and public works.

He also used religious tolerance and alliances to consolidate his power. Though Theodoric was an **Arian Christian** (those who believed Jesus was not divine), he tolerated all other Christian sects, and was a protector of the Jews. As marriage alliances were important in the politics of the time, Theodoric aligned himself by marriage to Clovis I, the great Frankish king, by marrying his sister. Nevertheless, Clovis desired to rule all the Goths, and Theodoric was forced into intermittent warfare with the Franks. He also engineered alliances with Visigoths, Vandals, and Burgundians.

One of the acts that Theodoric most bitterly regretted was hastily ordering the brutal execution of **Boethius**—"the last of the Romans." Boethius was a philosopher and government official who tried to rescue the intellectual heritage of the ancient Greeks and Romans through translations of the works of Aristotle and others. Boethius was imprisoned and executed without a trial for an alleged plot against the throne.

A quarrel between his Roman subjects and Pope John I over the edicts of Emperor Justin I against Arianism marred the end of Theodoric's reign. After his death, the Emperor **Justinian I** (see no. 17) ordered the Ostrogoths removed from Italy, and his forces drove them across the Alps to an unknown end.

**Theodoric receiving the keys to Ravenna**

23

# 17. Justinian I
## (A.D. 482–565)

During his nearly 40-year reign, the Emperor **Justinian I** strengthened and enlarged the **Byzantine Empire**, and he is remembered for codifying all existing Roman laws.

Born into a family of peasants in present-day Turkey, Justinian was brought to Constantinople by his uncle, Justin, who commanded the imperial bodyguard of the Byzantine Emperor Leo I. As a young man, Justinian was well educated in the Greek and Latin languages, and then took up a military career. When his uncle became emperor, Justinian served as his advisor. Justin legally adopted his nephew, marking him as heir and successor to the throne.

**Justinian and his Council**

In A.D. 525, Justinian married **Theodora**, a reputed beauty and former actress who became his lifelong, invaluable ally and advisor. When Justin died in A.D. 527, Justinian became emperor, and Theodora empress. Soon after, Justinian made major administrative changes and increased state revenues at the expense of his subjects.

The burden of Justinian's taxation policies, and the strong opposition of a dissident Christian sect, produced the widespread **Nika** riot in Constantinople in A.D. 532. With much of the city burning and parts of his palace destroyed, Justinian decided to flee. Empress Theodora, however, persuaded him to stand his ground; Justinian's forces rallied and before it was over, the rebellion had been put down, at the cost of more than 30,000 lives. With his power firmly established, Justinian now turned his attention to the West.

Justinian considered it his duty to regain provinces previously lost to the empire. During the A.D. 530s and 540s, he dispatched his generals to recover lands in Africa from the Vandals and Italy from the Ostrogoths. By A.D. 563, he reigned over all of the Roman Empire of Constantine the Great (see no. 13) except for Britain, Gaul, and parts of Spain.

Justinian's greatest accomplishments, though, came through his work as a codifier and legislator. Under his direction, the jurist Tribonian and his staff completed a ten-year compilation of all existing Roman law. It gave unity to the centralized state, and greatly influenced all subsequent legal history.

Justinian also instituted a large-scale program of public works, erecting a great number of buildings in many cities. Among his accomplishments was the building of the **Church of St. Sophia**, the supreme masterpiece of Byzantine art, which stands today as a museum in Istanbul.

Throughout his reign, Justinian not only relied on the counsel of the Empress Theodora; he allowed her widespread influence as well. She was devoted to social justice, particularly for women and children. During her reign, divorced women gained more rights, and children could not be sold to pay off their parents' debts.

After Justinian's death in A.D. 565 his nephew, Justin II, succeeded him.

# 18. Al-Mansur
## (c. A.D.714–775)

Al-Mansur firmly established the Islamic **Abbasid** dynasty, which ruled an empire that stretched from Spain to Baghdad (present-day Iraq) during the height of Arab civilization.

Al-Mansur was born in al-Humaymah, the home of the Abbasid family after their emigration from the Hejaz in A.D. 687–688. The family claimed they were descendants of al-Abbas, the uncle of **Muhammad**, the founder of Islam. Therefore, they asserted, they were the true heirs to his rule and the true leaders of the Arab world.

With this claim, the Abbasids led a coalition of Perisans and Iraqis in a revolution that toppled the first Islamic rulers, the **Umayyad** dynasty, in A.D. 750. Abbas al-Saffah, al-Mansur's brother, became the first Abbasid caliph (ruler). When he died in A.D. 754, al-Mansur undertook the task of establishing the Abbasid dynasty.

A number of revolts by ambitious army commanders threatened al-Mansur's caliphate. The most serious of these was the revolt in A.D. 754 of al-Mansur's uncle, Abdallah, the governor of Syria, who thought he had better claims to the caliphate than his nephew. The rebellion was only thwarted with the help of Abu Muslim, one of the chief organizers of the revolt against the Umayyads.

Al-Mansur was largely responsible for cutting the Abbasids free from the movement that had brought them to power. While his brother was still caliph, al-Mansur was involved in the murder of several leading personalities in that movement. Upon becoming caliph, one of his

**The Muslim Empire A.D. 750**

first acts was to bring about the death Abu Muslim, the man who had helped him retain power. These acts served both to remove potential rivals, and to dissociate the Abbasids from their "extremist" supporters.

During al-Manusr's reign, force was also used to repulse foreign invasions from the Byzantines (A.D. 758), annex new territory in Tabaristan (A.D. 759), and put down revolts in Iraq and Medina (A.D. 762). However, the crowning accomplishment of al-Mansur's reign, and his lasting legacy, was the construction of the city of **Baghdad** in A.D. 762.

The city was built in the form of a circle, with the Great Mosque and the caliph's palace—symbolizing the close association of religious and political power—located at the center. The new capital was also built to house the rapidly growing bureaucracy that al-Mansur, under the influence of Iranian ideas, developed to provide a stable basis for Abbasid rule.

Al-Mansur lived a life of simplicity and was a lover of poetry and a patron of the arts. He encouraged the translation of Greek and Latin texts into Arabic. He died in A.D. 775 on his way to **Mecca** for a pilgrimage, and was buried near that holy city.

# 19. Charlemagne
## (c. A.D. 742–814)

The reign of **Charlemagne**, the greatest European ruler of the **Middle Ages**, represented the merging of German, Christian, and Roman traditions, the essential characteristics of medieval civilization.

Born in Aachen in present-day Germany, Charlemagne (French for Charles the Great) was the grandson of Charles Martel (A.D. 689–741), famous for halting Arab expansion into Europe at the Battle of Poitiers in A.D. 732. In A.D. 768, upon the death of his father, Pepin the Short, Charlemagne inherited the northern half of the Frankish kingdom, while his brother, Carolman, inherited the southern half. When Carolman, died in A.D. 771, Charlemagne became sole ruler.

From the A.D. 770s through the 790s, Charlemagne fought many battles against various enemies, and succeeded in extending his father's kingdom to eventually include all of continental Europe except Spain, Scandinavia, southern Italy, and the Slavic fringes of the East. Peaceful relations with eastern Muslims and the Byzantine Empire were maintained through embassies and gifts.

**Charlemagne**

Charlemagne ruled his vast empire with the cooperation of noble families who received lands and booty for their help. He appointed counts and military governors to rule various parts of his realm; he also sent out royal messengers, usually one nobleman and one churchman, on annual journeys to supervise the execution of his laws and to keep an eye on other officials.

By the end of the eighth century, Charlemagne had established a royal palace at Aachen, and become very wealthy. His long-held desire had always been to rule an empire as vast as the old Roman Empire; at the same time, the Roman Catholic pope was looking for a single, dominant monarch who would rule Europe and protect and serve Christendom. As a result, Charlemagne found himself in Rome on Christmas Day, A.D. 800 being crowned "**Emperor of the Romans**" by Pope Leo III. For the next 14 years, Charlemagne would control more land and people than any European leader since the fall of the Roman Empire more than 300 years before.

Though a crude and rough man, Charlemagne was a patron of literature, science, and art. Among the prominent scholars at his court was **Alcuin of York**, leader of the palace school. These scholars helped create the "**Carolingian Renaissance**;" knowledge of Latin was renewed, and books were copied using the "Carolingian minuscule," the first script to use upper and lower-case letters, punctuation, and word spaces.

Charlemagne crowned his only surviving son, Louis the Pious, his co-emperor and sole successor at Aachen in A.D. 813. A few months later, the old king died. Although his empire survived him by only one generation, he had established a common intellectual, religious, and political tradition on which later centuries could draw.

**Alfred the Great** founded the English navy and repelled countless Danish invasions to keep his homeland free and the center of **Anglo-Saxon** law and tradition.

Alfred's birthplace was Wessex, one of the small, independent states of south England. At his birth, it was unlikely that Alfred would ever rise to king because he had three older brothers in line for the crown of their father, Ethelwulft, king of the West Saxons. However, all three had short lives and reigns, and Alfred eventually became king.

The greatest danger for the Anglo-Saxons people at this time was the raids of their lands by the **Danish**. In A.D. 870, the Danes threatened the entire Anglo-Saxon kingdom, consisting of Wessex, Mercia, Northumberland, and East Anglia. Alfred aided his brother, King Ethelred, in commanding the forces of Wessex. At the **Battle of Ashdown** in A.D. 871, they defeated the Danish army; but, their victory proved temporary and further defeats followed. When Ethelred was slain in battle later in A.D. 871, Alfred became king.

In A.D. 868, Alfred had married Elswith, a descendant of Mercian royalty. As king, he forged good relations with the other Anglo-Saxon kingdoms. He also built new forts in Wessex, strengthened older ones, and built the first English ships, preparing for more battles with the Danes.

In A.D. 876, a temporary peace ended, and the Danish leader **Guthrum** brought his army into Wessex, capturing many towns and causing Alfred to flee to a small fort in the marshes. However, from there Alfred was able to gather his forces, and two years later they won a great victory at the **Battle of Edington**. The Danes who surrendered were baptized as Christians, and the Treaty of Wedmore was signed bringing peace. The Danish King Guthrum honored the treaty until his death in A.D. 891. During the remainder of Alfred's reign, he defeated subsequent Danish invasions—skillfully using the navy he had built—until the Danes were forced to give up any attempt to conquer Wessex.

Alfred was a leader in government as well as in war. He organized the finances of the realm and the services due from his thanes (noble followers). King Alfred founded the civil structure of England, dividing the lands into shires, hundreds, and tithings. He also established a legal code, based upon his that of his predecessors.

**Alfred the Great**

A religiously devout and pragmatic man, Alfred recognized the general deterioration in learning and religion caused by the Danish destruction of monasteries. He arranged for, and took part in, the translation of books from Latin into Anglo-Saxon.

He died in A.D. 899, and was buried in Winchester, the resting place of the West Saxon royal family. His son Edward succeeded him.

# 21. Otto the Great
## (A.D. 912–973)

A dominant figure in early medieval Europe, **Otto I** established a strong kingship in Germany and founded the **Holy Roman Empire**.

Otto was the son of King Henry I, of Saxony, known as Henry the Fowler. Otto was not formally educated, but in his early years he received trained in hunting, horsemanship, and the use of arms. In A.D. 930, he married Edith, daughter of the English King Edward the Elder.

Although he was called king, Otto's father was actually first among equals of five German dukes who ruled Saxony, Franconia, Swabia, Bavaria, and Lorraine. Henry nominated Otto to succeed him, and in A.D. 936, a month after Henry's death, the German dukes elected Otto his successor.

Otto was determined to turn Germany into an empire. He did away with the independent duchy of Franconia, taking it for himself. By cooperating with the Christian Church he was further able to consolidate his power. He treated the German bishops as if they were counts or dukes, giving them land and titles. In return, they owed allegiance to him, and provided him with knights and soldiers in times of war.

Within the first three years of his rule, Otto was faced with threats from enemies both foreign and domestic, including some from his own family members. After he put down numerous uprisings, Otto then enjoyed 12 years of relative peace. By A.D. 950, he

**Otto the Great**

managed to bind all five independent German duchies to his crown. Though members of his family ruled over the duchies, Otto always kept a close eye on his empire.

After A.D. 950, the greatest external threat to Otto's empire came from the **Magyars**, a fierce warrior tribe from present-day Hungary. They invaded Germany in A.D. 954, ravaging the towns and countryside and murdering the citizens. In A.D. 955, Otto soundly defeated the Magyars at the **Battle of Lechfeld**, near Augsburg. This victory permanently ended the invasions from the East, and earned Otto the title "Otto the Great."

His next venture concerned Rome. Otto cultivated good relations with the papacy, and in A.D. 962, Pope **John XII** crowned him Holy Roman Emperor, a title that had previously only gone to descendants of Charlemagne (see no. 19). When Otto made several campaigns into Italy to acquire new lands, the pope turned against him. Otto used his influence in Italy to have the pope deposed and replaced him with his own candidate, who became Pope **Leo VIII**.

As Otto's kingdom expanded, the resultant flowering of culture, referred to as the **Ottonian Renaissance**, helped foster advances in learning and the arts. When Otto I died in A.D. 973, he left behind a united German empire.

# 22. Stephen I
## (c. A.D. 975–1038)

In the space of a generation, **Stephen I** went from pagan tribal leader to **Christian** leader of a powerful nation.

Stephen was a member of the **Arpád** dynasty, which came to rule the **Magyar** tribe in present-day Hungary around the end of the ninth century. Son of the Magyar chieftain Geza, Stephen married Gisela, daughter of Duke Henry II of Bavaria (present-day Germany) in A.D. 996. When Geza died the next year, the young man became leader of the Magyars.

Stephen I followed his father's attempts to Christianize his people, but he took a more direct approach. The young king asked Pope Sylvester II to baptize him and crown him king of Hungary; according to tradition, Stephen was crowned king on Christmas Day, 1001. With this action Hungary entered the spiritual community of the Western world; at the same time it reduced the possibility that the Holy Roman Emperor might assume the role of feudal lord over Hungary and make the Hungarian ruler his vassal. With the exception of an invasion by the Holy Roman Emperor Conrad II in 1030, and minor disputes with Poland and Bulgaria, Stephen's reign was peaceful.

Stephen then set about converting his people to **Christianity**, using force if necessary. He founded bishoprics and abbeys and made the construction of churches mandatory. He also encouraged his nobles to endow monastic foundations and schools and sent missionaries throughout his realm.

In 1018, Stephen and the Byzantine emperor, Basil II, defeated in battle the Bulgarian ruler John Vladislav. This victory allowed for the establishment of pilgrimage routes that would pass through Bulgarian lands on the way to Constantinople to the final destination of Jerusalem.

With the help of the clergy Stephen broke the power of the tribal chieftains, took over their lands, and appointed counts to administer them. He promoted agriculture and trade, and organized a standing army. He also organized a large frontier defense, consisting of swamps and forests, protected by regular frontier guards.

Under Stephen, the many tribes, as cohesive units, disappeared, but the fundamental social stratification was not altered. The privileged class was still make up of descendants in the male line of the old conquerors, answerable only to the king or his representative, and entitled to appear in general assemblies. Additionally, the landed classes were allowed to keep their slaves, although Stephen freed his own. The state only required members of this class to be ready for military service at any time.

Stephen died in 1038 with no direct male heir; he was succeeded by his nephew Peter Orseolo. Stephen was later canonized and became the patron saint of Hungary.

**Stephen I being baptized**

# 23. Canute the Great
## (c. A.D. 995–1035)

The Danish king **Canute** united the **English** and **Danish** people, and was the first person since the fall of Rome to rule over all England.

Canute was the son of Sweyn Haroldson, the king of Denmark, and Gunhild, a Polish princess. Though the couple was not legally married, Sweyn made Canute an heir.

For years the Danes had been raiding the kingdom of England. Sweyn I, invaded England again in 1009, and by 1013, with Canute accompanying him, Sweyn had subdued all of northern and eastern England. In the meanwhile, Ethelred II, the king of England, fled to Normandy, and Sweyn replaced him. Upon Sweyn's death in 1014, Ethelred returned to become king once more. Ethelred died in April 1016, and was succeeded by his son, Edmund II Ironside.

After much warfare between Edmund and Canute, the two rulers reached an agreement called the **Compact of Olney**. England was divided between the two; Canute received Mercia, London, and Northumbria, while Edmund kept Wessex. Edmund died shortly thereafter, and by 1017, Canute had been acclaimed king of all England. He quickly married Ethelred's widow, Emma, thus removing the danger of support for her surviving sons. Before the marriage took place, he stipulated that his two sons by his consort Elfgifu of Denmark would succeed to the English throne before those of Emma.

Canute's first actions were ruthless; he rewarded his Danish followers with English estates and he brought about the death of Edmund's brother Eadwig. Yet Canute did not rule solely as a foreign conqueror—he used both Englishmen and Danes as advisors. He used English support against external dangers, and also to secure his position in Denmark when he went there to take over the throne upon his brother's death in 1019. It would be some years later, in 1028, when after more than 3 years of fighting, he conquered Norway and became king. Through warfare, diplomacy, and tact, Canute had gained a widespread empire that ranged over thousands of miles.

Denmark and Norway were governed by regents Canute had chosen while he remained in England. There he was an effective ruler, bringing both internal peace and prosperity to the land. English trade profited by their king's control of the Baltic trade route. He won the trust of many of his English subjects by sending the main body of his army home to Denmark; he kept behind only 3,000 bodyguards. Probably under the influence of Archbishop Wulfstan, Canute also became a supporter of the Church. His law code, which Wulfstan drafted, was mainly based on those of earlier kings.

Canute died from illness at Shaftesbury, England in 1035.

**Canute the Great**

# 24. William the Conqueror
## (c. 1027–1087)

The man who crossed the English channel and conquered **Anglo-Saxon** England, was born in Falaise, Normandy (present-day France).

Born around 1027, William was the illegitimate son of Duke Robert I of Normandy, and Herleva, the daughter of a wealthy tanner. Before going on pilgrimage, Robert had asked the Norman barons to recognize his son William as the new duke of Normandy if he should die. When Robert died on the return journey in 1035, the barons complied with his wish. There was much upheaval during William's minority. His two guardians were murdered and anarchy reigned.

William finally asserted his powers in 1047, when King Henry I of France defeated Normandy's rebellious vassals. William also laid claim to the English throne, based on his assertion that his distant cousin, the childless English King **Edward the Confessor**, had promised him the throne in 1051. However, when Edward died in 1066, the Anglo-Saxon *witan* (high council) awarded the throne to **Harold Godwinsson,** who was more closely related to Edward.

Unwilling to accept this rejection, William gathered an army of Norman knights and crossed the English Channel on September 28, 1066. His 7,000 man force landed unopposed at Pevensey, England, and began building fortifications at **Hastings**.

King Harold had been occupied to the north, fighting an invasion of Danes. With his forces exhausted after defeating the

**William the Conqueror**

invaders at the Battle of Stamford Bridge near York, Harold hurried to meet William. Harold marched his army some 250 miles in nine days, gathering inexperienced reinforcements to replenish his weary men as he advanced.

In the lengthy and exhausting battle that followed, William made skillful use of his archers and cavalry against the English infantry. When Harold was killed, the demoralized English forces fled.

William then led his army all the way to London. The Archbishop of Canterbury crowned William **King of England** on Christmas Day 1066.

Under William's rule, the Anglo-Saxon witan was dissolved and replaced with a royal council, who advised the king on financial, judicial, and military affairs. William allowed the church to retain its lands, but he retained the appointment of bishops and important abbots. In addition, by royal decree church jurisdiction and lay jurisdiction were separated, and the bishops were given their own courts. This was a decisive step in the evolution of common law as an independent force in England.

Numerous military campaigns, together with an economic slump, prompted William to order an investigation into the actual and potential wealth of the kingdom to maximize tax revenues. The quickness and efficiency of this survey was remarkable for its time, and the result was the two-volumed **Domesday Book** of 1086, which still exists today.

William died in September 1087.

# 25. Frederick I (Barbarossa)
## (c.1123–1190)

King of Germany and Italy, and Holy Roman Emperor, **Frederick Barbarossa** restored order in Germany, then spent 30 years trying to restore the glories of the Roman Empire.

When his father Frederick, Duke of Swabia (in present-day southwest Germany), abdicated in 1147, Frederick succeeded him. Then when his uncle, the Holy Roman Emperor Conrad III, died in 1152, Frederick was elected king of Germany. A strong, handsome man with golden hair and a red beard, Frederick was energetic, highly intelligent, and a leader of men.

**The death of Frederick Barbarossa**

During his reign, Frederick was kept busy on two fronts: organizing his German feudal estates and keeping the nobility satisfied with concessions, honors, and consultations, and restoring imperial authority in Italy.

In 1152, Frederick declared a general peace of the land in Germany. It was enforced with the help of ministers, whom he selected from his entourage, instead of the nobility or church as was the custom. He was then crowned king of Italy, after capturing and turning over to Pope **Eugene III** the reforming monk, Arnold of Brescia, in 1154. Eugene III also crowned Frederick Holy Roman Emperor. Frederick now considered himself heir to the tradition of rulers such as Justinian (see no. 17) and Charlemagne (see no. 19), and aimed at restoring the power and glory of the Roman Empire.

Frederick was concerned with expanding and consolidating royal lands. In 1156, he wed Beatrice, heiress of the county of Burgundy, thereby regaining Burgundian lands through marriage.

Frederick then tried to subdue northern Italy; he took the **Lombard** cites, including Milan. Pope Alexander III, attempting to hold Frederick back, excommunicated him in 1160. Frederick did not make peace with the pope until 1176, after the emperor had met with defeat in northern Italy at the hands of armies supported by the pope.

Frederick's many expeditions into Italy weakened his authority at home. Trouble came in the form of Duke Henry the Lion, a Bavarian noble who wielded power in both Bavaria and north Germany. However, by 1179, Frederick was able to confiscate Henry's holdings and send him into exile.

When Pope Clement III convinced Frederick to participate in the **Third Crusade** in 1189, the Holy Roman Emperor was joined by **Richard the Lionhearted** of England and **Phillip II Augustus** of France. This campaign was to be Frederick's last—he drowned while trying to cross the swift currents of the River Salef in Cilicia (present-day Turkey) in 1190. Before his journey, Frederick had secured the crown for his son, Henry VI, whom he also succeeded in marrying to the heiress of the kingdom of Sicily and southern Italy.

# 26. Saladin
## (1137–1193)

**Saladin** was a **Muslim** leader who united the Arab world and fought the combined royal forces of Christianity in the **Third Crusade** near the end of the 12th century.

Born in Tikrit, Mesopotamia (present-day Iraq), Saladin was the son of a military officer and administrator. At age 14, he was sent to Aleppo, in northwest Syria, to be trained under his uncle Shirkuh, an advisor to Nur-ad-Din, the leader of the armies of the Muslim caliphate of Baghdad.

In 1164, Saladin accompanied his uncle and the forces of Nur ad-Din on a campaign in Egypt, which was ruled by the rival Fatimid caliphate. In 1169, after his uncle's death, Saladin became vizier (a high government official); under his administration local revolts were suppressed, Cairo was fortified, and several public works were begun. In 1171, Saladin abolished the Fatimid caliphate, and was proclaimed the **Abbasid** caliph in Egypt.

In 1174, when Nur ad-Din died, Saladin stretched his forces and took control of Syria. He now had command of not only Egypt and Syria, but also the Hejaz (in present-day western Saudi Arabia), Yemen, and the coastal portion of Libya. Only the emperor of Byzantium was more powerful. This position allowed Saladin to consider an attack on the Christian-held land that lay between Egypt and Syria: **Palestine**, which the Christians had conquered during the First Crusade (1095-1099).

During the 1180s, Saladin initiated holy war against the Christians, and gathered a cavalry and infantry force of more than 20,000 soldiers. One of the greatest battles came in July, 1187, in Palestine at the **Horns of Hattin**. Saladin's forces won a complete victory, and, with the surrender of Jerusalem, 88 years of Christian domination had ended. In victory, Saladin showed a combination of

**Saladin**

both brutality and benevolence. He had all the Christian Knights Templar executed, but allowed the Christian population to ransom itself with payments of gold.

However, Christian Europe could not accept this new Muslim takeover of the **Holy Land**. In 1191, forces under the command of monarchs Richard the Lionhearted from England and Philip II Augustus from France arrived to fight Saladin in a Third Crusade.

The Crusaders laid siege to Acre, a seaport city in present-day Israel, and after a lengthy fight, the city surrendered. Philip sailed for France, and Richard pressed on in the fight to reclaim Jerusalem. He was unsuccessful though, and after numerous battles, a three-year truce was arranged in September 1192, that left Jerusalem in Arab hands, but allowed Christian pilgrims the right to visit the city.

Saladin returned to Damascus, where he died in 1193.

Under Pope **Innocent III** the Catholic Church reached the height of its prestige and power in medieval times. He instituted the **Fourth Crusade**, convoked the historic **Fourth Lateran Council**, and asserted widespread papal influence over the political affairs of Christian Europe.

Born **Lothario de Segni**, the young man studied theology and canon law, and rose steadily through Church ranks with the help of family connections. When Pope Celestine III died in 1198, de Segni was unanimously elected to succeed him.

Innocent III was immediately confronted with the insecurity of papal sovereignty in the papal states. He soon had partial success in regaining papal rights, bring such states as Spoleto, Ancona, and Romagna under control, while others such as Florence, Lucca, and Sienna retained their autonomy.

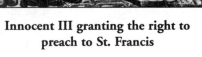

**Innocent III granting the right to preach to St. Francis**

Building on the work of Pope Gregory VII, Innocent asserted the right of the Catholic Church to intervene in the political affairs of Christian Europe. The decade-long struggle over the rightful heir to the title of Holy Roman Emperor ended with Innocent appointing his own candidate, Frederick II, as emperor and replacing German influence in Italy with his own. Innocent used his power of interdiction and excommunication to bring both England and France under his sway. In addition, he fostered canon law, which governed the conduct of clergy, monks, and nuns everywhere, exempting them from certain civil laws, thus reducing a king's power in his own domains.

Hoping to unite the Christian Church of the East with that of Rome, Innocent launched the Fourth Crusade in 1202 to take **Jerusalem** from the **Muslims**. The Crusaders, though, went against his wishes and sacked Constantinople—a move that caused further distracting wars, preventing an attack on Jerusalem.

Innocent also approved another crusade—this one against the French Albigensian heretics, who denied the sacraments and the authority of the Church hierarchy. Force, in the form of an **Inquisition**, along with massacres by papal armies, destroyed the Albigensians.

The Fourth Lateran Council, held in 1215, was the climax of Innocent's papal rule. Attended by 400 bishops, 800 abbots and priors, and representatives of all the monarchs of Christendom, its decrees were of tremendous significance for the Church. Among its accomplishments were a pronouncement that the Church was one and universal; an agreement on transubstantiation—the belief that the substance of the bread and wine of the Last Supper is changed into the body and blood of Christ; a denial of clerical participation in ordeals such trial by battle; and the institution of more rigorous rules for monastic life.

In the midst of vast preparations for new Crusade that he hoped would liberate the Holy Land, Innocent died suddenly, in 1216.

# 28. Philip II (Augustus)
## (1165–1223)

Perhaps the outstanding figure of his time, **Phillip II** of France consolidated the power of the monarchy through his leadership skills, and by the end of his reign, his kingdom had emerged as an organized state.

Philip, was the son of Louis VII of France and his third wife, Adela of Champagne. He was a member of the seventh generation of **Capetian** rulers. In 1179, when Philip was only 14, his father fell gravely ill; by the end of the year the young man had succeeded to the throne.

Philip inherited a small kingdom, consisting mainly of Paris and the surrounding area, known as the Ile-de-France. To increase his holdings, in 1180 Philip married Elizabeth of Hainaut, an important territory in Flanders. Through her dowry Philip gained Artois, a northern French county, as well as Amiens and Vermandois.

In 1190, Philip joined Richard the Lionhearted of England and set out on the Third Crusade. However, before he reached the Holy Land, Philip turned around and returned to France, after quarreling with Richard and contracting the "sweating sickness" that permanently left him with a nervous and erratic temperament.

Philip was extremely concerned over the health of his young heir, Louis VIII. Philip's wife, Elizabeth, had died before he went on crusade; in order to secure the continuation of the Capetian line, he married the Danish princess Ingeborg in 1193. A day after the marriage, however, he sought an annulment. In 1196 he married Agnes of Meran and they had two children.

Philip had a strong desire to increase his land holdings. In 1199, England's Richard the Lionhearted died and was succeeded by his less-skilled brother John. Philip went on the

**The Battle of Bouvines, July 27, 1214**

attack, after three years of warfare, gained control of the English-held lands of Normandy, Brittany, Anjou, Maine, and Touraine, and incorporated them into his kingdom. During his reign, he quadrupled the territory directly controlled by the French king.

In 1214, Philip formed an alliance with **Frederick II**, the Holy Roman Emperor; together their forces defeated both John of England and Otto II of Brunswick (in present-day central Germany) at the **Battle of Bouvines** in Flanders. This victory simultaneously added more lands to Philip's kingdom as well as enhanced his prestige as a leading European monarch.

After this, Philip turned his energies to domestic affairs. He instituted reforms in law, and turned Paris into a major city by paving the streets, building and fortifying the walls of the city, and beginning the construction of the **Louvre Museum**. By the end of Philip's reign, Paris was becoming an artistic, intellectual, and political European capital.

Upon Philip's death in 1223, his son, Louis VIII, succeeded him.

**Genghis Khan**

The most feared conqueror in history, **Genghis Khan** united several **Mongol** tribes, formed them into an army, and led them on a campaign of terror and conquest to create the largest empire the world had yet seen.

Born with the name **Temujin** near the Onon River in present-day Mongolia, he was the son of Yesugei, chief of the Borjigin tribe of Mongols. When he was nine, his father died, and Temujin grew up on his own in a fierce environment of competing Mongol tribes.

As a warrior, Temujin set himself apart by combining skillful leadership in diplomacy and battle. Around 1206, the great assembly of Mongols named him "Genghis Khan," or supreme leader. Khan then proceeded to unite the Tatar, Kereit, Naiman and Merkit tribes into one fearsome army of Mongol warriors.

The Mongols swift rise to power came from Khan's dynamic leadership. While the Mongol tribes had long been renowned as warriors, Khan molded them into a much greater fighting force—disciplined, organized, ruthless. He picked his generals from among his sons or trusted allies; he was also an adaptable ruler, and had the ability to learn from others.

Khan mounted his first campaign against the **Chin Empire** in northern China. Even the Chinese defenses behind the Great Wall were no match for Khan's forces; they captured the great city of Peking (present-day Beijing) in 1215. From there, Khan turned his attention to the **Kharismian Empire** (present-day Afghanistan and Iran), capturing and sacking Samarkand, the center of the empire. Khan sent part of his army north where they entered southern Russia and defeated a large army led by the princes of Kiev. This defeat meant that Russia would be under the "Mongol yoke" for the next three centuries.

By the early 1220s, Khan's **Mongol Hordes**—as his heavily armed horsemen came to be known—had swept across northern China, over Azerbaijan, Georgia, and northern Persia. Khan's forces then conducted a campaign in northern India, destroying Muslim cities there before returning to Mongolia in 1224.

Then they set out again to invade and conquer China, this time attacking the **Hsi Hsia Empire**, located in north-central China. As this campaign was beginning, Khan fell from a horse, suffered internal injuries, and died a short time later. He was buried on a sacred hill in the Kentei Mountains in present-day Mongolia.

At the time of his death, Ghengis Khan had built the largest contiguous empire in the known world. His successor, his son Ogodai Khan (1185–1241), continued on a path of conquest, and the Mongol Empire would continue to grow until the end of the 13th century and the reign of Kublai Khan.

# 30. John (Lackland)
## (1167–1216)

King John's reign is remembered for both foreign and domestic crises, and for a baronial rebellion that led to the first "Bill of Rights" of English-speaking peoples—the **Magna Carta**.

John was the youngest son of King Henry II of England and Eleanor of Aquitaine. John, whom his brothers had nicknamed **Lackland**, because he had not received lands from his father, was, nevertheless his father's favorite, while Richard was favored by his strong-willed and powerful mother. As Duke of Aquitaine, Richard, supported by his mother, revolted against his father's rule twice, once in 1173-1174, and again in 1188-1189.

For reasons unknown, on the second occasion John deserted his father and sided with Richard. Henry died before he could mount a fight to defend his crown, and Richard became King **Richard I** (later called the Lionhearted).

When Richard took the crown in July 1189, he made John **Count of Mortain** (in northwest France), confirmed him as lord of Ireland, and granted him lands and revenues in England. In return for all he had received, John had to promise not to enter England when Richard decided to embark on the Third Crusade.

However, when John learned in January 1193 that Richard, returning from the crusade, had been imprisoned in Germany, he made an unsuccessful attempt to seize control of England. On Richard's return, John hid out in Normandy, but shortly thereafter threw himself on his older brother's mercy and was forgiven. John remained loyal to Richard until Richard's death in 1199, whereupon he assumed the throne.

John's reign was marked with crises. The first was the major loss of England's territories in France; **Philip II** took England's royal and baronial lands in Normandy, Anjou, Maine, and Brittany.

Finances were another concern. King John's inherited estates in England and western France were overburdened with debt. To raise revenues, he laid ever-increasing tax burdens on his barons, and extorted a loan of 66,000 marks from the Jews who lived in England.

The final crisis reflected baronial discontent with John's taxation and war policies, and arbitrary style of government. In 1215, his opponents presented him with a statement of his obligations in the form of a Magna Carta (the Great Charter). This document laid the foundation of English liberties and the basis of government by consent of the governed for much of Western civilization.

John's later repudiation of the agreement led to the first **Baron's War**, which ended only with the king's death in 1216. He was succeed by his nine-year old son, Henry III, who ruled under the guardianship of the Earl of Pembroke.

**John swearing revenge against the barons**

37

Robert the Bruce seized the Scottish throne and went on to lead **Scotland's** fight for independence from England. He stabilized both the Scottish monarchy and the nation.

Born in 1274 at Turnberry castle in southern Scotland, he was the son of Robert de Bruce VII, the earl of Carrick. When in 1286, Alexander III of Scotland died, both Robert de Bruce and **John Balliol** submitted their claims for the crown of Scotland to **Edward I** of England. Edward appointed Balliol to the kingship, but by 1296, Edward deposed Balliol because of an alliance he made with France. Edward then declared himself king of Scotland, which would then be governed by English administrators.

The English officials proved to be oppressive and harsh. When a knight named **William Wallace** rose up against the English, young Robert Bruce joined Wallace's forces, which went on to defeat the English at the **Battle of Stirling Bridge** in 1297. However, Edward prepared for further battle, and defeated Wallace's forces at the **Battle of Falkirk** in 1298, sending him into exile, and eventual capture and execution. Robert Bruce, who cooperated with the English forces this time, became joint administrator of Scotland, with Sir John Comyn of Badenoch, a nephew of Balliol.

In 1305, Bruce decided Scotland needed its complete freedom from England, and he became the leader in a new war of independence. In 1306, he or his supporters, murdered Sir Comyn, his rival for the crown; Bruce was then crowned King of Scotland at Scone on March 27, 1306.

Edward was enraged by Bruce's actions. The English met and defeated Bruce at the Battle of Methven in Perthshire, and Bruce became a fugitive. However, Edward's death in 1307, and the succession of his less effective son Edward II aided Bruce. He led a slow and determined effort to capture English fortresses and castles over the next several years. Then, against an English army nearly three times its size, Bruce's forces were victorious at the **Battle of Bannockburn**, in June 1314. Edward II was routed and nearly captured, and Bruce carried the war to northern England. Bannockburn was the turning point that confirmed the re-establishment of an independent Scottish monarchy. By 1323, England and Scotland had agreed on a truce, and in 1324, the pope recognized Robert as king of Scotland. While the English made further attempts to invade Scotland, Bruce repulsed them. Finally, they recognized his title and Scotland's independence in the **Treaty of Northampton**, signed in March 1328.

Robert Bruce's reign was brief; he became seriously ill and died in 1329. His son David II, succeeded him.

**Robert the Bruce**

As the first woman medieval ruler in Europe, **Margaret I** pursued policies that united **Denmark, Norway**, and **Sweden**, a tri-partite union that lasted for more than 130 years.

Margaret was a descendent of Canute the Great (see no. 23), and the daughter the Danish king Valdemar IV. When she was but six years old, Margaret was betrothed to Haakon VI, king of Norway. The 10-year-old Margaret wed 23-year-old Haakon in Copenhagen in 1363.

Margaret spent her youth under the tutelage of Märta Ulfsdotter, a daughter of the Swedish saint, Bridget, in Haakon's Norwegian court. An accomplished scholar, Margaret's early talent as a ruler soon overshadowed her husband's, and she appears to have exercised the real power. The couple's only child, **Olaf**, was born in 1370.

After her father's death in 1375, Margaret successfully had Olaf elected to the Danish throne and ruled in his name. Following her husband's death in 1380, the Norwegian crown also passed to Olaf, with Margaret again ruling in his name. The Danish-Norwegian union that was to last until 1814 had begun. Then Margaret and Olaf, who came of age in 1385, were poised to make war on **Albrecht** of Sweden and claim the Swedish throne—when Olaf died in 1387. Using her diplomatic skills, Margaret became ruler of both Norway and Denmark and, in the absence of an heir, adopted her six-year-old

**Margaret I**

grand-nephew, **Erik of Pomerania**. Joining with Swedish nobles who were resentful of Albrecht granting favors to the Germans, Margaret was eventually proclaimed Sweden's "sovereign lady and rightful ruler." She defeated Albrecht in 1389, though his supporters did not surrender Stockholm until 1398.

Margaret now ruled all three **Scandinavian** states. Her heir, Erik of Pomerania, was proclaimed hereditary king of Norway in 1389 and of Denmark and Sweden in 1396. Margaret retained the actual rule of Scandinavia until her death. She aimed to further develop a untied Scandinavian state with its center at Denmark and consolidated her administration through a network of royal sheriffs. To strengthen herself economically, she levied heavy taxes and reclaimed church estates and lands in Denmark and Sweden that had once belonged to the crown.

Margaret also succeeded in foreign affairs. She used diplomatic means to achieve her main goals—to end German expansion to the north and to extend and secure Denmark's southern borders. Armed conflict did, however, break out with Holstein in southern Germany. During this war, Margaret died, possibly from plague, in 1412. Though she left a united Scandinavia, she had strengthened Denmark at the expense of Norway and Sweden, a course of action that would eventually cause problems. Her adopted heir Eric succeeded her.

A member of the family that dominated the powerful Italian city-state of **Florence** for three centuries, **Lorenzo de Médici** was a statesman, politician, and patron of the arts who exerted enormous influence during the height of the **Renaissance.**

The son of Piero de Médici and Lucrezia Tornabuoni, Lorenzo was a very bright young man; he was elected to the Council of One Hundred, the main ruling body of Florence, when he was only 17 years old. Following in the footsteps of his Médici relations, Lorenzo cultivated many political allies and friends. In June 1469, he married Clarice Orsini, of a Roman noble family, further enhancing his power and prestige. When his father, Piero, died in 1469, Lorenzo became head of the Médici family; he ruled Florence jointly with his brother Giuliano.

The Médici's fortunes were in banking and other commercial pursuits. Lorenzo's humanist training, however, left him ill-prepared to supervise all the banking branches, both inside and outside Italy. He was forced to rely on managers, several of whom did not serve him well. As new competitors sprung up throughout Europe, he found his power being challenged.

His most formidable rival, the **Pazzi** banking family, formed a conspiracy, with Pope **Sixtus IV**, among others, to overthrow his family. The Pazzis decided to assassinate Lorenzo and his brother Giuliano in the cathedral during Easter mass. Giuliano was killed, but Lorenzo was only wounded, and managed to flee.

When Lorezno retaliated and the subsequent **Pazzi War** (1478–1480) broke out, the pope excommunicated him and issued an interdict on Florence. However, Lorenzo eventually negotiated a settlement and emerged with greatly increased prestige. He then created a Council of Seventy, replacing the old Council of One Hundred, with himself in complete control of the new governing body. Under his leadership, a 12-year period of peace ensued among the several rival Italian city-states.

A collector of antiques, Lorenzo himself contributed more than anyone to the flowering of Florentine genius during the second half of the 15th century. He bought ancient Greek and Latin manuscripts, which he then had copied. Additionally, he encouraged the use of Italian in writings whereas Latin had been the language of literature.

Toward the end of his life, Lorenzo opened a school of sculpture in his garden of San Marco, where he came to recognize the early genius of a 15-year-old pupil; the young student was **Michelangelo**, and Lorenzo commissioned many of the great artists' early works. Lorenzo's health began to decline about three years before his death. He died at age 43, and his eldest son, Piero, succeeded him.

**Lorenzo de Médici**

# 34. Ferdinand II
## (1452–1516)

Through inheritance and by marriage, **Ferdinand II** brought Spain's two main kingdoms under a joint rule and laid the foundation for the country's status as a world power.

Ferdinand was the son and heir to the throne of King Juan II of **Aragon**. In 1469, he married his cousin, **Isabella I**, the half-sister of King Henry IV of **Castille** and the heir to his throne. In 1474, Isabella succeeded to the Castilian throne, and she and Ferdinand assumed joint rule. In 1479, Ferdinand succeeded his father as king of Aragon, and all of Spain, except for the kingdom of Granada, fell under the rule of both monarchs.

From 1475 to 1479, Ferdinand took a firm hand in Castile with his young wife to transform the kingdom politically. He revised the town charters, making the towns the center of resistance to feudal aggression in the interest of royal order and authority. At the same time, royal confiscations of property did much to increase the crown's finances.

Ferdinand also banned all religions other than **Roman Catholicism**. In 1478, the **Spanish Inquisition**—a dark chapter in Spanish history—enforced this ban and bolstered religious and political unity. However, in the process, thousands of people were tortured and killed. In 1492, Ferdinand recaptured **Granada** from the Moors, bringing the remaining part of Spain under his rule. The Moors were given the choice of becoming Catholics, or being exiled. That same year, Ferdinand also expelled from the kingdom all Jews who refused to accept Christianity—perhaps as many as 200,000 people. These measures of expulsion deprived Spain of two groups that had provided valuable cultural, intellectual, and economic communities.

**Isabella and Ferdinand**

Spain's era of expansion and imperialism took a giant leap forward when in 1492, Ferdinand and Isabella sponsored the first of **Christopher Columbus's** voyages of exploration across the Atlantic. They would lead to the establishment of many Spanish colonies in the **New World** and the growth of Spain's international reputation.

Isabella died in 1504, and Ferdinand married Germaine de Foix, a niece of the king of France. Ferdinand began Spain's struggle with France for control of Italy in the **Italian Wars** and conquered Naples in 1504. In 1512, he annexed most of Navarre, basing his claim on his marriage to Germaine de Foix. After Isabella's death, he retained control over Castile as regent for his daughter Joanna.

For the rest of his life, Ferdinand continued his regency over Castile, first in the name of Joanna, who became insane, and then for his grandson, Charles V, who later became Holy Roman Emperor. When Ferdinand died in 1516, he left his grandson a united Spain, as well as Naples, Sicily, Sardinia, and an overseas empire.

Montezuma was the last emperor of the powerful **Aztec Empire**, which ruled present-day Mexico with a population of 11 million people before the Spanish Conquest.

Born around 1480, Montezuma was the sixth son of Axayácatl, ninth ruler of the Aztecs. Aztec civilization revolved around both religion and war, and the young Montezuma was trained as both priest and warrior. Religious ceremonies included human sacrifices, and this need for victims was a cause for continual warfare. The Aztecs ruled their vast empire more through fear than loyalty.

By 1509, Montezuma had expanded his empire to as far away as present-day Nicaragua. The capital city of **Tenochtitlán** (present-day Mexico City), was a city of massive buildings, orderly streets, and wide plazas. Its inhabitants had a written language and a very accurate calendar. Tribute in the form of cotton, gold, silver, jade, pottery, captives, and foods of all kinds poured into the emperor.

The year 1519 brought the beginning of the downfall of the empire. The Spanish conqueror **Hernán Cortéz** landed on the Aztec coast with an army of some 600 men. Aztec priests thought the arrival of this light-skinned man was the return of the legendary god, **Quetzalcoatl**, who, according to Aztec mythology was to return in the year 1519 to reclaim his empire. Montezuma sent ambassadors with gifts to greet Cortéz and his men; the Aztec leader hoped the treasures he sent would persuade them to leave. Instead, they made Cortéz determined to gain more riches.

Cortéz and his army marched to Tenochtitlán and entered the city in November 1519. Though some of Montezuma's advisors thought the strangers may be hostile, he believed Cortéz to be the long-awaited god. The Aztec ruler greeted him, and the Spaniards enjoyed great feasts, were given long interviews with the emperor, and allowed free reign of the city.

A week later, Cortéz took Montezuma hostage and forced him to negotiate a truce. The Spaniards occupied the city for months. In June 1520, the Aztecs, already angry at Montezuma and believing that he had become a puppet of Cortéz, revolted. Montezuma was killed and Cortéz's forces were driven out of the city. His small army might have been destroyed, but for an outbreak of smallpox—brought by the Spaniards—that killed many Aztec leaders.

Cortéz returned the following year, accompanied by a large army of Aztec-hating warriors from other tribes. The Aztecs put up a valiant fight, but after a 90-day siege of Tenochtitlán, Cortéz razed the great city to the ground, bringing an end to the Aztec Empire. When the city was rebuilt, it emerged as the capital for an empire called **New Spain**.

MUTECZUMA
*Rex ullimus Mexicanorum*

**Montezuma II**

42

# 36. Henry VIII
## (1491–1547)

The obsession with producing a male heir, caused **Henry VIII** to break with the Catholic Church, thereby changing the religious and political history of **England**.

Henry was the second son of Henry VII, the first English monarch from the House of Tudor. The young man was educated in the spirit of the Renaissance—he was fluent in six languages, a gifted musician, and a student of theology and mathematics.

Henry became heir to the throne after the untimely death of his older brother Arthur; in 1509, at the age of 17, Henry ascended the throne upon the death of his father. That same year, he married the first of his six wives, **Catherine of Aragon**, Arthur's widow.

For the first 20 years of his reign, Henry pursued a life of pleasure, leaving the affairs of state to his advisors, including his talented minister, Cardinal Woolsey. Henry's major concern was producing a male heir, and as Catherine reached middle age without giving birth to one, Henry tried to end their marriage so he could remarry. However, since the Catholic Church did not permit divorce, Pope **Clement II** refused permission. Henry was enraged and took steps to withdraw England from the Church of Rome.

In 1533, the king and his friend Thomas Cranmer, the new Archbishop of Canterbury, arranged for Parliament to declare that the Divine Right of Kings superseded the authority of the pope. They then withdrew England from Catholicism and created the **Church of England** (Anglican Church).

A further move, the **Act of Supremacy** in 1534, confirmed Henry as "Supreme Head of the Church of England." This act was the beginning of the **English Reformation**, and created the second major Protestant faith after Lutheranism, founded by Martin Luther in the 1520s. Eventually, Henry began to seize the church's wealth and its land, the sale of

**Henry VIII**

which helped sustain his financially troubled government.

In the meantime, Henry divorced Catherine in favor of **Anne Boleyn**, who gave birth to a daughter, **Elizabeth**, but no son. Henry soon grew tired and suspicious of Anne; he accused her of adultery, and she was executed in 1536. Henry then quickly married **Jane Seymour**, a lady at court, and she gave birth to a son, Edward. Jane died in childbirth, and Edward would grow into a sickly young man.

By the time of his death, Henry had married three more times, without producing another male heir. His only son Edward VI, succeeded him, but ruled for only six years. In the aftermath, there was a bitter struggle between Catholics and Protestants for control of England, until ironically, Henry and Anne Boleyn's daughter Elizabeth I came to power in 1558, and reaffirmed England's Protestantism.

The greatest ruler of the **Ottoman Empire**, Europeans called **Suleiman** "the Magnificent" for the brilliance of his court, but Ottomans knew him as al-Qanuni (the Lawgiver), because of his control of all aspects of daily life.

Born in Trebizond, in present-day, Turkey, Suleiman was the son of Selim I "The Grim," who had forced the abdication of his father, and murdered his two uncles and more than 60 other relatives. When Selim died in 1520, the 26-year-old Suleiman became sultan of the Ottoman Empire.

Suleiman was determined to advance the **Muslim** cause by making war on Christian Europe, and at the same time surpassing Holy Roman Emperor Charles V as the greatest ruler of their time. Suleiman began his conquests with the capture of Belgrade from the Hungarians in 1521. The following year, he drove the **Knights of St. John**, a religious order of soldier-monks, from the island of Rhodes. The knights had long used Rhodes to prey on Turkey's trade between Constantinople and Egypt. Suleiman's forces captured Rhodes using, along with the conventional weapons of war, bombs—the first time they were used in warfare.

In 1529, Suleiman laid siege to Venice, threatening all of Christendom. Though the defenses of Venice were inadequate and its forces insufficient, Suleiman's army was forced to withdraw because of the horrible weather.

**Suleiman I**

During the 1530s, Suleiman's navy, under the command of his grand admiral **Barbarossa** (Khair-ed-Din), engaged in warfare in the Mediterranean, while Suleiman marched his army eastward by land. They went on to Baghdad and fought a long series of campaigns against the **Persians** before reaching peace terms in 1555. Suleiman's final campaign ended in failure. An assault against Knights of St. John on the island of Malta in 1566 was thwarted by the bravery of the knights and the rocky terrain of the island. The Turks lost 20,000 men and many ships. Suleiman vowed to avenge the defeat but died later that year.

During Suleiman's lifetime, Constantinople had become a center for arts, with the creation of gem-studded jewelry, porcelain, textiles, and carpets. His architects created magnificent mosques in the great cities of his far-reaching empire. While the population of the empire had doubled to 22,000,000 under his rule, rural overpopulation led to mass migration to the cities, and hence unemployment, food shortages, and rising prices. Nevertheless, this great leader brought his nomadic state to the level of a global superpower at the dawn of the modern age.

After Suleiman's death, the Ottoman Empire began a slow decline from which it was never to recover. His son, Selim II "The Drunkard," succeeded him.

# 38. Charles V
## (1500–1558)

A ruler who controlled lands on three continents, Holy Roman Emperor **Charles V** fought a losing battle to keep his empire together under **Roman Catholicism** in the face of emergent Protestantism.

Charles V was born in Ghent, the Netherlands. Upon the death of his father, Philip I, in 1506, Charles inherited the Burgundian realm. Following the death of his maternal grandfather, Ferdinand II, in 1516, he became ruler of the vast Spanish kingdom; and when his paternal grandfather, Maximilian, died in 1519, he gained the Hapsburg lands in central Europe. That same year, after having bribed the electors, Charles was chosen king of Germany. At the age of 20, he was the most powerful sovereign in Christendom.

The following year brought many changes. In the spring, Charles summoned the German monk **Martin Luther** before the **Imperial Diet at Worms** to defend his *95 Theses*, Luther's attack on the Catholic Church that eventually ignited the Protestant Reformation. When Luther refused to recant his views, Charles had him banned and he declared war on Lutheranism.

That same year, Charles began the first of his many wars with **Francis I** of France. By 1525, Charles's troops soundly defeated those of the French monarch. In a peace agreement the following year, Francis renounced all claim to Milan, Genoa, and Naples, as well as lands in Flanders, Artois, and the duchy of Burgundy. While Charles was increasing his control over European lands, Hernán Cortés was conquering the rich Aztec Empire (present-day Mexico) and accumulating those lands in North America for Spanish control under Charles's rule. In 1533, Spanish conquests would spread to South America with the destruction of the Inca Empire in Peru.

In 1530, Charles was crowned Holy Roman Emperor by the pope. For much of the remainder of his reign, he was engaged in a war against the **Ottoman Turks**, as well as a battle to crush the growing Protestant movement in Germany. By the 1550s, Charles had become tired of all the fighting, so he ordered all the Catholic and Protestant German princes to assemble in the city of Augsburg. There in 1555, a settlement was reached which called for the religion of each German state to be decided by its ruler.

While Charles accepted this agreement, he was not pleased with it, because it did not provide for the religious unity he spent years trying to achieve. Weary of the reigns of power, he abdicated his claims to the Netherlands, Italy, and all of Spain and its possessions in favor of his son **Philip II**, and the rule of the Holy Roman Empire to his brother Ferdinand I. Charles retired to a monastery, where he died in 1558.

**Charles V**

Champion of the **Roman Catholic Counter-Reformation**, **Philip II** ruled Spain during the height of its power, his empire stretching throughout Europe across the Atlantic Ocean to North and South America.

Philip was the son of the Holy Roman Emperor Charles V (see no. 38) and Isabella of Portugal. As a young man, he had an enlightened education. At the age of 16, he was married to the first of his four wives, his cousin Maria of Portugal, who died in childbirth. His other wives were Mary I of England, Elizabeth of Valois, and Anna of Austria.

**Philip II**

On the abdication of his father in 1556, Philip became king of Spain. He succeeded to all his father's dominions except Germany. The title of Holy Roman Emperor and the ancient Hapsburg lands went to Philip's uncle, Ferdinand I.

During his reign, Philip engaged in many costly wars that tested the strength of his empire. The fourth and last **Hapsburg-Valois War** was decisively concluded when he defeated the French at St. Quentin in 1557, and at Gravelines the following year. In 1559 , the **Treaty of Cateau-Cambrésis** firmly cemented Spanish hegemony in Italy. Philip also fought the **Muslim Turks**, who threatened Spain's rich possessions in Italy and the Mediterranean; a Spanish fleet achieved a great victory against the Turks at the Battle of Lepanto in 1571.

In 1580, when the last male heir to the Portuguese throne died, Philip laid claim to the crown through what he considered his hereditary rights; his mother Isabella was the daughter of King Manoel I. Philip was supported by the high clergy and part of the nobility, and that, combined with his military forces, helped him secure the crown.

Though Philip was a conscientious ruler, he was a devout Catholic to the point of fanaticism, and was intent in stamping out **Protestantism**. When his second wife, Mary Tudor—the Catholic queen of England—died in 1558, he asked for the hand of her half-sister, Elizabeth I, who succeeded to the throne. However, Elizabeth refused his proposal and returned England to the Protestant Anglican Church founded by her father, Henry VIII (see no. 36).

Unable to forge an alliance with England through marriage, angered by its Protestantism, and jealous of its growing naval power, Philip launched an ill-fated attack against England in 1588. Spain's massive Armada—132 vessels and more than 3,000 cannon—were defeated by the English, and much of its fleet was scattered by a major storm.

Although the defeat damaged his empire and diminished Spanish prestige, when Philip died in 1598, Spain was still at the height of its power. He was succeeded by his son Philip III.

# 40. Elizabeth I
## (1533–1603)

Under the reign of **Elizabeth I**, England became an established international power, achieving economic prosperity, and ushering in a cultural awakening where literature and the arts flourished as never before.

The daughter of King **Henry VIII** (see no. 36) and his second wife, Anne Boleyn, Elizabeth hardly knew her mother. When she was only three years old, her mother was charged with adultery and beheaded. After the execution, her parents' marriage was invalidated, and Elizabeth was declared illegitimate. However, in 1544, the Act of Succession restored her in line for the throne after her half-brother Edward and her half-sister Mary.

By the 1550s, there was bitter conflict between **Catholics** and **Protestants** in England. Elizabeth's older half-sister, Mary, now England's Catholic queen, had Elizabeth imprisoned in the Tower of London and then exiled because Mary feared Protestant leaders might try to place Elizabeth on the throne. However, when the queen neared death, she reconciled with Elizabeth and named her as successor.

In 1558, the 25-year-old Elizabeth became queen; it was soon apparent that she was more than equal to the job. Using intelligence, wit, and caution, she chose able and wise advisors, who helped her steer England on a steady and prosperous course. On religious affairs, she reverted England to Protestantism, but took a moderate approach. She established the Anglican Church's separation from Rome, but based the church 's structure on the Catholic model. As long as her subjects attended the Anglican Church, they were not persecuted for their private beliefs.

Throughout her rule Elizabeth was determined to avoid alliances with other monarchs through marriage. Despite pressure from Parliament, she refused all proposals and

**Elizabeth I**

declared herself to be the **Virgin Queen**. Later in her reign, Elizabeth's rule was threatened by supporters of her Catholic cousin, **Mary Queen of Scots**. Mary had been living in England under house arrest for 19 years, after she was forced to abdicate the Scottish throne. In 1587, when Mary was implicated in yet another Catholic plot against the queen, Elizabeth signed her death warrant and she was executed.

Elizabeth also faced threats from foreign powers, especially Spain, which was fast gaining power throughout Europe and the world. In 1588, **Philip II** of Spain sent an "invincible" Armada to invade the small island. However, England's fleet soundly defeated the Spanish forces, which were later nearly completely destroyed when a storm scattered what remained of its fleet.

During her reign, Elizabeth stabilized England's finances by introducing a new currency. Her rule was also a time of unparalleled literary achievement, where such renowned writers as **William Shakespeare** flourished.

When Elizabeth's 45-year reign ended, the popular and dynamic queen was mourned by the whole nation.

The most famous of all French kings, **Louis XIV** led France through an age of political, military, and cultural ascendancy in the Western world.

Born in 1638, the future king was not yet five years old when his father, Louis XIII, died. Until he came of age, Louis' mother, Anne of Austria, ruled as queen regent, but power actually resided with the chief minister, Cardinal Mazarin. In 1660, Louis XIV married Maria Theresa, daughter of Philip IV of Spain. The following year, on the death of Mazarin, the 23-year-old Louis announced that he himself would govern. For the next 54 years, the **Sun King**—so called for the flamboyant brilliance of his court—ruled as an absolute monarch.

The first 20 years of the king's reign were the most successful. The finances of the kingdom were reformed, trade increased, and a strong colonial policy undertaken. The French army became the finest fighting machine in Europe. Theater, music, architecture, painting, sculpture, and the sciences flourished.

In 1682, Louis turned **Versailles**, the enchanting chateau of his youth located just outside Paris, into the official residence of the court and seat of French government. By pro-viding enough space to house the courtiers (court attendants), the chateau and its out-buildings helped to domesticate the nobility. Devoting himself to his people, Louis put himself constantly on public display. The wheels of the administration established during the early part of his reign ran smoothly. At the center, the king and council decided; in the provinces, administrators executed the king's orders. The courts were entirely under Louis' control.

During his coronation, Louis had sworn to defend the Catholic faith. To preserve the religious unity of his kingdom, he launched a struggle against the growing Protestant followers of John Calvin known as **Huguenots**. In 1685, Louis rescinded the **Edict of Nantes**, which had decreed religious tolerance. The forced conversions and persecutions that followed led to the emigration of some 200,000 Huguenots.

In a series of wars between 1667 and 1697, Louis extended France's eastern border at the expense of the Hapsburgs. However, the last years of his reign brought troubles. In the **War of the Spanish Succession** (1701–1714), Louis engaged a hostile European coalition, which feared French domination in Europe, to secure the Spanish throne for his grandson, Philip of Anjou. While Louis was ultimately successful, the war drained France's finances and effectively checked French expansion in Europe.

By 1715, a series of deaths in the royal family left the king's five-year old great-grandson as the heir to the throne. Despite the brilliance of his reign, Louis XIV left behind a nearly bankrupt and militarily weakened France.

**Louis XIV with playwright Jean Molière**

# Peter the Great
## (1672–1725)

Czar **Peter the Great** transformed Russia into a modern state, creating a new capital, building a navy, and expanding his nation's borders to gain important access to the Baltic Sea.

Peter was born in Moscow in 1672, the son of the Czar Alexis Mikhailovich Romanov and his second wife, Natalia Naryshkin. With the death of Alexis in 1682, came a bloody struggle for the succession between the families of his first and second wives. The result was that Peter and his half-brother Ivan were made co-czars, while Peter's half-sister Sophia served as regent.

**Peter founding St. Petersburg**

In 1689, Peter managed to remove his sister from her position. Upon Ivan's death in 1696, Peter was officially declared Czar of all Russia.

A huge and imposing figure at six foot, seven inches tall, Peter was both energetic and inquisitive, generous and cruel. From the beginning of his reign, he set out to modernize Russia, which at the time had no navy, no ports, and conducted no trade or exchange with other European countries. In 1697, he embarked on a European tour, at times traveling incognito, to acquire the Western techniques necessary to modernize both Russia's armed forces and its industry. After returning home, he Europeanized Russian court life, bullying his nobles into cutting their beards and adopting Western dress. The Church became subservient to the state, and the old

Russian calendar was changed to the Western Julian calendar.

In the late 1690s, Peter imported ship-builders from Austria and Prussia to construct warships and other vessels for a Russian navy; this fleet allowed him to capture the Turkish fortress on the Sea of Azov and build a Russian naval station there. Peter then began a war against Sweden for control of lands on the edge of the Baltic Sea. In the first battle of the **Great Northern War** (1700–1721), Russia suffered a crushing defeat at the hands of the Swedes and their brilliant military leader, King **Charles XII** at the **Battle of Narva**.

Following this disaster, Peter began extensive reform to modernize the Russian army by hiring architects and engineers to bring in artillery and train his men. In 1704, Peter captured Narva in a siege, and in 1709 won a decisive victory at the **Battle of Poltava**. The **Treaty of Nystad**, concluded in 1721, gave Russia the eastern shores of the Baltic, Peter's desired "window to the West."

Peter used some of the conquered Swedish territory to build a new Russian capital along the Neva River; the city of **St. Petersburg** would eventually spread to all the surrounding islands serving the river's tributaries.

Peter died in February 1725 after a brief illness and was succeeded by his wife, Catherine.

Brilliant military commander and enlightened monarch, **Frederick II** turned his small north German kingdom of Prussia into one of the most powerful states in Europe.

Frederick was the son of Frederick William I, king of Prussia, and Sophia Dorothea of Hanover, daughter of England's King George I. In May 1740, Frederick succeeded his father as king. Later that year, Austria's ruler, Charles VI, died and was succeeded by his daughter, **Maria Theresa**. Frederick used the opportunity to seize Silesia, a rich Austrian province with an advanced economy.

Frederick's actions instigated the **War of the Austrian Succession** (1740–1748), during which Frederick often played both sides, changing allies and enemies with great skill and duplicity. When the war ended, he still held Silesia—as well as the undying hatred of Maria Theresa and her most formidable ally, Empress Elizabeth of Russia.

Beginning in 1757, France, Sweden, Russia, and many of the smaller German states joined against Frederick in the **Seven Years' War** (1756–1763). For Frederick, the

**Frederick the Great**

war soon became a life-and-death struggle. As the forces he could put in the field dwindled and his subjects resisted the unprecedented burdens of the war, the Prussian position became increasingly difficult; by 1761 it was desperate.

The death of the Russian empress, Elizabeth, in January 1762, changed the situation. Her successor, her nephew Peter III, who fanatically admired both Prussia and Frederick, signed an armistice in May followed by a Russo-Prussian peace treaty. Maria Theresa's hopes of recovering Silesia were now ended. The 1763 **Treaty of Hubertusburg** left the province in Frederick's hands. Prussia had survived, its military reputation was greater than ever—but not without cost. The army had lost 180,000 men, and some provinces had been completely devastated. Thereafter, Frederick was determined to avoid another such conflict.

Frederick's wars established his personal reputation as a military genius and won recognition for Prussia. Besides Silesia, Frederick also acquired East Frisia on the North Sea coast and later, at the First Partition of Poland in 1772, he obtained West Prussia, thus forming a territorial link between East Prussia and the rest of his domains to the west.

In contrast to his reputation as a ruthless and ambitious military leader, Frederick was also a man of culture and a patron of literature and the arts. He was interested in the new **Enlightenment** movement sweeping Europe. He invited the great French writer **Voltaire** to Berlin, and even wrote poetry himself. He also made agricultural and industrial improvements, and pursued a policy of religious tolerance. Among his other reforms, Frederick revised and modernized the judiciary, and issued a new codification of Prussian law.

Reformer and humanitarian, **Maria Theresa** of Austria was one of the 18th century's greatest woman rulers.

Maria was born in Vienna in 1717, the eldest daughter of Emperor **Charles VI**. In 1736, she married Francis Stephen of Lorraine and the marriage was a love match. The couple had 16 children, 10 of whom survived to adulthood.

Before his death in 1740, Charles VI, with no male heir, altered Hapsburg family law by an edict called the **Pragmatic Sanction** under which Maria Theresa would inherit and rule his vast holdings. Upon his death, she became Queen of Hungary and Bohemia, and archduchess of Austria. However, when she ascended the throne, her subjects were discontented, the army weak, and her foreign enemies eager to exploit the situation.

Her claim to the throne was challenged, and she soon became embroiled, in the **War of the Austrian Succession** (1740–1748). By the end of the war, she had lost most of Silesia, a land rich in ore deposits, to **Frederick II** of Prussia. She was also forced to give up lands in Italy to both Spain and Sardinia. However, with the **Treaty of Aix-la-Chapelle** in 1748, her rights to the throne were acknowledged, and her husband was recognized as emperor.

After the war, the empress turned toward domestic matters and financial reforms. Agriculture, manufacturing and commerce began to flourish once more, and national

**Maria Theresa**

revenues increased, while taxes were lowered. She appointed ministers to reorganize her armies and skillfully handle foreign affairs.

Even with these successes, Maria Theresa never accepted the loss of Silesia. In 1756, she allied herself with France and Russia against Prussia, resulting in the **Seven Years' War**, which exhausted Europe and left the territorial position essentially as before.

When the Seven Years' War ended in 1763 and left the monarchy with a mountain of debts, Maria Theresa became a champion of peace, a reformer and a humanitarian. Her reforms included education, introduction of public health services, codified laws, and the abolishment of torture. Deeply pious, she nevertheless began to move toward subordinating the Church to the authority of the state. Her reign was considered the most moral in Europe.

Her husband's death in 1765 plunged Maria Theresa into prolonged grief, and caused her to turn to her son Joseph, who served as co-regent during the final 15 years of her life. However, a continuous conflict with Joseph clouded the years of her widowhood. She mistrusted his interest in the Enlightenment, and was offended by his admiration of Frederick the Great. Ironically, her own reforms smoothed the road for the enlightened despotism that was to mark Joseph's reign as her successor.

As empress of Russia, the energetic and resourceful Catherine greatly extended her nation's borders, and continued the modernization begun by Peter the Great at the beginning of the 18th century.

Born in Stettin, Prussia (present-day Poland), her birth name was **Sophia Augusta Frederica**, daughter of a prince of Anhalt-Zerbst; she later adopted the name Catherine upon conversion to the Orthodox faith. As a young girl, she was summoned to Russia by Empress **Elizabeth I** in the hopes of a marriage arrangement to Elizabeth's nephew Peter, the grandson of Peter the Great, and the heir to the throne. The young couple married in 1744, but the marriage was not a happy one.

**Catherine the Great**

In 1762, Peter ascended the throne. However, his unstable nature, and pro-Prussian sentiments made him very unpopular. After a six-month reign, Peter was overthrown in a military revolution led in part by **Grigori Orlov**, Catherine's lover, who was conspiring to put her on the throne. Peter was murdered shortly thereafter, and in September 1762, Catherine's 34-year reign began.

In foreign affairs, Catherine wanted to expand her empire. As a result of two separate wars with Turkey (1768–1774 and 1787–1791), she gained control of the **Crimea** and access to the Black Sea. She also annexed a vast amount of territory on Russia's western border by taking part with Prussia

and Austria in three separate partitions of Poland (1772, 1793, and 1795).

In domestic affairs, Catherine intended to make Russia a prosperous and powerful state. To replenish the state treasury, she secularized the property of clergy, who owned one-third of the land and serfs. The Russian clergy became powerless state-paid functionaries. Many of her actions favored the nobles, whom she needed for support. She excused them from military service and expanded their rights over their serfs, a situation that led in 1773 to a massive peasant revolt, which was crushed by the military.

Catherine was influenced by reading the works of the **Enlightenment**, and sought to make Russian society as cultured as that of Paris and Berlin. She corresponded with French writers such as **Voltaire**, brought experts to court to collect art and antiquities, and turned **St. Petersburg** into one of Europe's cultural centers.

Catherine was a brilliant, forceful ruler who worked tirelessly—she often arose at 5:00 a.m. and worked 15 hours a day—and she did much to modernize her country. She reorganized the 29 provinces, built hundreds of new towns and renovated old ones, expanded trade and developed communications, and established both medical schools and the first schools for girls.

When she died in 1796, Catherine was succeeded by her son, Paul I.

# 46. George Washington
## (1732–1799)

Leader of the Continental Army in America's fight for independence, **George Washington** was the overwhelming choice of the new nation's founders to become the first president of the United States.

Born in Westmoreland County, Virginia in 1732, he was the son Augustine Washington, a Virginia landowner. Washington's father died when he was 11 years-old, and he attended school irregularly until he was 15, when he left to become a surveyor. He inherited **Mount Vernon** at the age of 20, and became head of one of Virginia's largest estates.

In 1753, he took an oath as a major in the Virginia militia. At age 22, he commanded the first British forces in the **French and Indian War**, rising to rank of colonel, and continuing his command until the end of the war.

As a plantation farmer, he soon became prominent in community affairs, and in 1758 he was elected to the Virginia House of Burgesses. In 1759, he married **Martha Dandrige Custis**, who brought her own wealth and land holdings to the marriage.

Washington was serving with the Virginia militia at the start of the **American Revolution** (1775–1783) when the newly formed Continental Congress named him commander-in-chief of the **Continental Army**. Washington's troops won many hard-fought campaigns, including a daring and brilliant attack across the Delaware River that smashed the British forces at Trenton and Princeton. Final victory was achieved with the British surrender at **Yorktown** in 1781, and after two years of negotiations, a peace treaty was signed in 1783.

After the war, Washington retired to his Virginia plantation at Mount Vernon. However, he was called upon to preside over the Constitutional Convention in 1787, which drew up the Constitution of the United States. Two years later his countrymen unanimously elected him the **first president** of the United States.

As president, Washington tried to govern by consensus, relying on his top Cabinet appointees, such as Secretary of State **Thomas Jefferson** and Secretary of the Treasury **Alexander Hamilton**. This was often difficult, as those two men rarely agreed on government policy. Washington was reelected in 1793, and during his eight years in office, Vermont, Kentucky, and Tennessee joined the Union, the Bank of the United States was chartered, and the national mint was established.

Washington could have served another four-year term had he wished to, but he refused. In March 1797, he gave his farewell address in which he urged Americans to avoid the fighting brought on by rival political factions and to remain free of foreign entanglements. His brilliant military and political leadership was crucial to the foundation of the young nation.

**George Washington**

# 47. Louis XVI
## (1754–1793)

**Louis XVI** ruled France during its most tumultuous period, and his inability to deal with the **French Revolution** cost him his crown—and his life.

Louis was born at Versailles, outside Paris, the grandson of Louis XV and third son of the Dauphin (the heir to French throne). The deaths of his father and his two elder brothers made the young prince the Dauphin in 1765. In 1770, he married 15-year-old **Marie Antoinette**, youngest daughter of Archduchess Maria Theresa of Austria.

On Louis's accession to the throne in 1774, France was burdened with debts; heavy taxation spread misery among the people. Louis immediately remitted some of the most oppressive taxes and instituted financial reforms. His attempts to enact reforms met with general approval. However, his poor judgment left him unsuited to provide the leadership needed to control the complex social and political conflict smoldering in France.

In May 1776, Louis appointed Jacques Necker director of the treasury, but costly French intervention in the American Revolution undermined his efforts. Necker resigned in 1781, and those who followed him were unable to ward off bankruptcy. Louis then convoked the Assembly of Notables and asked their consent to tax the privileged classes, but they refused.

Louis finally convoked the **States-General** (assembly) in 1789, but he opposed the suggestion that the number of deputies from the third, or popular estate, be doubled. This led

**Louis XVI**

to the third estate proclaiming itself a **National Assembly**. It renamed itself the Constituent Assembly and drew up a new constitution, declaring that political independence, equal rights, and universal freedom were inviolable rights.

Louis sent troops to Paris and rumors circulated that the king intended to suppress the assembly. This provoked the storming of the **Bastille** on July 14, 1789, and ignited the French Revolution.

At first Louis seemed inclined to work with the revolutionaries, trying to convince the people that he favored republican principles. However, the queen and Louis's advisors influenced him to disregard all promises and flee to Austria to fight the revolution from there. The royal family fled to Versailles, and in October 1789, a crowd attacked Versailles and forced them to return to Paris.

During the next two years, the king alternately made concessions to the revolutionaries and made plans to escape from them. The queen tried to enlist help from her brother, the emperor of Austria. When the royal family attempted to flee France in disguise, they were apprehended and brought back as political prisoners.

In September 1792, the National Convention declared France a republic. Louis was brought to trial, convicted of treason, and sentenced to the guillotine. He was executed on January 21, 1793. His wife, Marie Antoinette, met the same fate later that year.

# 48. Napoleon Bonaparte
## (1769–1821)

One of history's greatest generals, **Napoleon Bonaparte** transformed the French Revolutionary Republic into an empire and conquered much of Europe.

He was born on the island of Corsica, the son of a lawyer and prominent official. Napoleon studied at military schools in France, and at 16, he joined the artillery as a second lieutenant, and rose rapidly within the ranks.

After suppressing a royalist uprising in Paris in 1795, Napoleon was given command against the Austrians in Italy. Before he left, he married **Josephine de Beauharnais**, widow of a noble executed during the Revolution. Their marriage would later end in divorce because she could not provide him with children and an heir.

By 1798, Napoleon had become a general, and he led an invasion of Egypt to strike at Britain's colonial empire. He also had become immensely popular in France. When he returned in 1799, he overthrew the **Directory**, the weak government running the country. He then established a new constitution calling for a **Consulate**, and named himself first consul. By 1804, a vote by the people declared him emperor.

Between 1804 and 1812, Napoleon forged the largest European empire since Charlemagne (see no. 19). One by one, his enemies fell; the Russians and Austrians at Austerlitz in 1805; the Prussians at Jena in 1806, and the Austrians again at Friedland in 1807. By 1810, Napoleon controlled France, Poland, Italy,

and every country in between, including Austrian and the German states of the Holy Roman Empire.

In some of the foreign lands he controlled, Napoleon secured the reigns of power for his relatives. He occupied Portugal, and placed his brother Joseph on the Spanish throne. In exchange for not being annexed to France, Holland accepted his brother Louis as monarch.

Napoleon's ambitious attempted conquest of **Russia** in 1812 was the beginning of his downfall. He defeated the Russians at **Borodino**, but they burned Moscow before he could occupy it. When severe winter weather threatened the French supply lines, Napoleon was forced to retreat. The battered army returned home with only 50,000 men left out of 600,000.

This disaster encouraged Prussia and Austria to declare war again in 1813. Despite his brilliant campaign on French soil, the allies invaded Paris and compelled him to abdicate. Napoleon was banished to the island of **Elba**; however, he escaped in March 1815, and took power again for 100 days. Britain and Prussia then led an alliance against him and he was defeated at the **Battle of Waterloo**, in Belgium in June. He surrendered to the British, and abdicated once again.

Napoleon spent the remainder of his life in exile on the island of **St. Helena** in the South Atlantic Ocean.

**Napoleon**

55

Known as "the Liberator," **Simón Bolívar** succeeded in freeing much of South America from the yoke of Spanish colonialism, but saw his dream of a continent of several states united under one banner end in bitterness and sadness.

**Simón Bolivar**

Simón Bolívar was born in 1783 in Caracas, Venezuela, at the time part of the Spanish empire of South America. The son of a wealthy **Creole** family, Bolívar was educated in Madrid, and then traveled in Europe, where he witnessed the French Revolution and the rise of Napoleon. These events made a deep impression on him, and he vowed to try to free his homeland from Spanish rule.

Bolívar returned home and helped lead a revolutionary movement that deposed the viceroy of Caracas in 1810. However, Bolívar was later forced to flee, and established himself in Cartagena, in present-day Colombia. From there, he wrote his famous *Cartagena Manifesto*, an impassioned plea for a strong central government and a professional military to free his people from Spanish rule.

For the next nine years, Bolívar made several attempts to reconquer Caracas and liberate Venezuela, alternately meeting with success, but then being driven off by Spanish forces. In July 1819, Bolívar led his forces on an historic crossing of the Andes mountains and in August they won the decisive **Battle of Boyaca**. Installed as dictator of Venezuela, he then set out to liberate New Granada (present-day Colombia) and Quito (present-day Ecuador). By 1822, he had accomplished both; he then combined Venezuela with both states and formed the new **Republic of Gran Colombia**, with himself as its first president.

Bolívar continued his efforts to drive the Spanish from the entire continent. By 1825, his forces had removed them from Peru, and when he freed upper Peru, it was renamed **Bolivia** in his honor. The following year he created a Bolivian constitution, and named himself president for life.

In 1826, Bolívar tried to form a Great Convention of South American states, but it met with failure. He was reelected president of Colombia, but opposition was beginning to grow from some people who feared he wanted to create an empire and rule like Napoleon. In 1828, he was forced to suppress a rebellion that threatened his rule and his life.

In 1830, first Venezuela and then Quito withdrew from the Republic of Gran Colombia. Bolívar, now bitter with resentment, resigned as president of the fractured nation and retired to Cartagena.

Simón Bolívar had spent his entire life—and much of his own considerable inherited wealth—fighting for the independence of the South American people. Shortly before his death, he wrote a farewell message complaining of ingratitude and defending himself against charges of personal ambition.

# 50. Shaka
## (c.1787–1828)

**Shaka** was a Zulu chief who established the first **Zulu Empire** in southern Africa and created a fighting force that devastated the entire region.

The illegitimate son of a minor Zulu chieftain and an orphaned princess, Shaka became a top soldier in the **Mthethwa** confederacy, one of the small chiefdoms located in South Africa between the Drakensburg Mountains and the Indian Ocean. A protégé of the Mthethwa chieftain Dingiswayo, Shaka became more powerful than his sponsor; in 1816, he claimed the Zulu chiefdom for himself.

At this time, the Zulus probably numbered fewer than 1,500. Shaka immediately increased and reorganized the Zulu fighting force, turning it into a formidable military machine geared to total warfare. He forced young tribesmen to leave civil society and form a permanent army. He armed them with short stabbing spears and instilled in them a strict military discipline almost unknown in tribal peoples. As his warriors conquered new regions and peoples, Shaka absorbed the conquered men and boys into his own forces, a tactic that greatly increased their numbers. At its height, the army included around 40,000 men.

By 1820, Shaka had command of most of southeast Africa and present-day Natal. Although he limited his assaults to the coastal area, they indirectly led to the **Mfecane** (the Crushing) that devastated the inland plateau in the early 1820s. Marauding clans, fleeing the Zulu wrath and searching for land, destroyed the clan structure of the African interior and left two million people dead in their wake.

By the mid-1820s, Shaka had created a single kingdom out of the tribes and confederacies between the Tugela and Pongola rivers. He ruled as a despot. His word was law, and his emphasis on military matters created a nation that was maintained by use of force.

In 1827, Shaka's mother died, and he became openly psychotic. In grief, he ordered 7,000 Zulus killed. He became increasingly dictatorial and cruel. He practically ordered his clan to death by starvation in reverence to his mother. For more than a year no crops were planted and milk was not allowed to be used.

Early in 1828, Shaka sent his army south in a raid that carried the warriors clear to the borders of the Cape Colony. Instead of allowing the warriors to rest when they returned, he sent them off on another raid far to the north. His actions were too much for his army, and two of his half-brothers murdered him in September of that year. Shaka's descendants ruled the Zulus for another 50 years, until British forces won the Zulu War (1879) and created 13 small states from the Zulu kingdom.

**Shaka**

One of Great Britain's most skillful 19th century statesmen, **Benjamin Disraeli** played a key role in government affairs during the height of the British Empire's power and influence.

The son of English author Isaac D'Israeli, he was born in London, of Italian-Jewish descent. His father's decision to convert his entire family to **Christianity** in 1817 was crucial to Disraeli's career—Jews were excluded from Parliament until 1858.

Disraeli enjoyed a private education and was trained as an attorney. However, after falling into debt as a young man, he turned to writing. His first novel, the somewhat biographical *Vivian Gray*, brought him fame in 1826, but his later work was less commercially successful.

During the 1830s, Disraeli decided to enter politics. He joined the **Conservative party** (the Tories), and after failing twice, finally won a seat in the House of Commons in 1837.

Disraeli was an active parliamentarian, but when Conservative Robert Peel became prime minister in 1841, Disraeli did not receive a

**Benjamin Disraeli**

position in his government—a slight that he never forgot. After a dispute within the party in 1845, Peel resigned, and Disraeli succeeded him as head of the Tories.

During the 1850s, Disraeli twice served as chancellor of the Exchequer (equivalent to U.S. secretary of the treasury) in the government of **Edward Derby**. However, after Disraeli's Parliamentary reform measure failed in 1858, he resigned, and was part of the opposition for several years while the Liberals were in power.

He became chancellor again in 1866 in a third Derby administration, and succeeded in getting his **Reform Bill** of 1867 passed; it redistributed Parliamentary seats and greatly increased the number of voters. When Derby resigned because of ill health in 1868, Disraeli became prime minister. He resigned, though, after the Liberals won the general election later that year. His bitter enemy, **William E. Gladstone**, then became prime minister.

When the Conservatives came to power again in 1874, Disraeli became prime minister once more. During his tenure he profited from the friendship of **Queen Victoria**, a political conservative who disliked Gladstone.

Disraeli was most influential in foreign affairs, where he fostered Britain's imperialism. He secured a loan of £4,000,000 to enable Britain to purchase a controlling interest in the **Suez Canal**, a vital waterway linking Europe with India and the Far East. He annexed the Fiji Islands in 1874 and the Transvaal (northeast South Africa) in 1877. Early in 1876, Disraeli, arranged for Queen Victoria to be crowned Empress of India, solidifying that country's role as the "crown jewel" of Britain's empire.

Disraeli's term as prime minister ended when the Conservatives met with defeat in 1880. By this time, his health was poor, and he died in London the following year.

Revered as one of Mexico's greatest political figures, **Benito Juárez** became the first Native American president of his country.

Juárez was born in the Mexican state of Oaxaca into into a **Zapotec** Indian family. He practiced as a lawyer in his native state and served as state governor from 1847 to 1852. After being imprisoned in 1853 for his opposition to **Santa Anna**, Mexico's dictator, Juárez spent a period of exile in the United States. He then returned to Mexico and became a key figure in the Liberal revolution that overthrew Santa Anna in 1855.

As minister of justice under the new government, Juárez attacked the special privileges of the army and Church. He wrote many reforms into a new constitution, drawn up in 1857. These measures separated Church and state, ended Church ownership of land, and required that cases involving the clergy and the army be tried in the regular courts. However, opposition to the new constitution was strong among Conservatives, and in 1858, the Mexican president resigned and fled the country.

Juárez stepped in as acting president, but soon he and his followers were forced to flee to **Veracruz** where they set up their own government. The Conservatives then established a rival government in Mexico City, and three years of civil war ensued. In the end, the Liberals won, culminating in Juárez being constitutionally elected president.

Many serious problems faced the new president, including an almost empty treasury. To restore some financial stability, Juárez decided in July 1861 to suspend payment of foreign debts for two years. This action angered England, Spain, and France, and by January 1862, the three countries had troops at Veracruz. However, when Britain and Spain realized that Napoleon III of France was planning to conquer Mexico and control it through a puppet government led by

**Benito Juárez**

**Archduke Maximilian** of Austria, they withdrew their forces. Napoleon succeeded in his efforts as the French occupied Mexico City in June 1863. Soon after, Maximilian took control of the government.

Forced to leave Veracruz, Juárez retreated to El Paso del Norte (present-day Ciudad Juárez) at the Mexican-U.S. border. In 1865, the United States, which had refused to recognize Maximilian and supported Juárez, demanded the withdrawal of French troops, citing a violation of the Monroe Doctrine. Under pressure, Napoleon withdrew his troops in early 1867, allowing Mexican forces to capture and execute Maximilian.

Juárez then restored order, returned to Mexico City, and was reelcted president in December, 1867. Juárez's last years were marked by controversy and poor health. Still, he ran again for president in 1871 and was reelected, but he died of a heart attack the next year.

**Giuseppe Garibaldi**

Italian patriot and revolutionary leader, **Giuseppe Garibaldi** was the driving force behind the 19th century movement to unify Italy for the first time since the days of the Roman Empire.

Born in Nice, in present-day France, Garibaldi came from a family of seafarers. Garibaldi went to sea at the age of 15, and by the time he was 25, he was a master of his own ship. Within two years, he also found a cause which was to consume him for the rest of his adult life—the fight to liberate and unify Italy.

At the time, Italy consisted of several small principalities and dukedoms controlled mostly by Austria. **Giuseppe Mazzini** (1805–1872) had formed the Young Italian Society, with a call to liberate and unify Italy, and it was this movement that Garibaldi joined. An uprising in Genoa in 1834 failed, and though Garibaldi escaped, he was sentenced to death in absentia by the Sardinia-Piedmont government.

Garibaldi fled, first to French territory, and then he made his way to South America, where he fought alongside rebels trying to liberate Uruguay. In 1848, Garibaldi returned home as the Italian people rose up again to overthrow their foreign rulers.

In 1849, he led his troops in an heroic struggle in Rome that lasted for weeks against the French, Austrian, and Neapolitan armies. When they could no longer hold out, Garibaldi and his men escaped in a daring march that brought them fame throughout Italy.

Garibaldi once more went into exile. He made his way to the United States and lived quietly for a while in New York. He returned to Europe in 1854 and settled on Caprera, a desolate island off of Sardinia.

In May 1860, Garibaldi sailed from Genoa with 1000 men, his famous **Redshirts**. They landed on the island of Sicily, and using guerrilla tactics Garibaldi had learned in South America, they completely routed the 25,000 man army of Naples. Throughout the summer, Garibaldi's forces marched across Sicily and then north, crossing the Straits of Messina, onto the mainland, winning one victory after another.

By mid-September, when Garibaldi marched into Naples, he had become the virtual dictator of Sicily and southern Italy. He then magnanimously yielded all his power to King **Victor Emmanuel II** of Sardinia-Piedmont, who thereby became king of a united Italy, except for Venice and Rome.

Garibaldi then retired to Caprera, a hero to millions. He fought again in 1866 to take Venice away from Austria, and then served in his nation's parliament from 1874 to 1876. He died at Caprera in 1882 and was mourned by all of Italy.

# 54. Abraham Lincoln
## (1809–1865)

Leader of his nation during its darkest hours, **Abraham Lincoln** rose from humble origins to become savior of the Union and one of America's greatest presidents.

Abraham Lincoln was born in a log cabin in the backwoods of Hodgenville, Kentucky. Despite little formal schooling, he taught himself both grammar and mathematics. After his family moved to Illinois, Lincoln tried a variety of occupations. He then entered politics, was elected to the Illinois state legislature in 1834, and served until 1843.

During this time he also turned his studies to law and opened a practice. In 1842, he married **Mary Todd**, and four years later, he was elected to the U.S. House of Representatives. He served one term before returning to Illinois to resume his law practice.

The repeal by Congress in 1854 of the Missouri Compromise, and the reopening of the debate on the extension of slavery in new U.S. territories drew Lincoln to politics again. He joined the new **Republican party** in 1856, and two years later became their candidate for the U.S. senate from Illinois, opposing the incumbent, Democrat Stephen Douglas. The candidates engaged in a series of debates and although Lincoln lost the election, he established a national reputation.

In 1860, the Republicans, pledged to oppose the extension of slavery, chose Lincoln as their presidential candidate. The Democrats nominated two candidates— John Breckinridge of Kentucky, and Lincoln's senate opponent, Stephen Douglas. With the antislavery northeast and midwest solidly behind him, Lincoln won the election convincingly.

In February 1861, a month before Lincoln took office, 11 southern states left the Union and formed the Confederate States of America. Lincoln's attempt to resupply the federal garrison at Fort Sumter, South Carolina, precipitated a Confederate attack against the garrison and ignited the **Civil War**.

During the four-year struggle, Lincoln attacked the vast problems of the war with vigor and skill. By 1862, he was convinced the Union cause would be even further strengthened by a bold political move. So he issued the order emancipating all slaves in states engaged in rebellion, a turning point in the nonmilitary side of the conflict. However, the preservation and restoration of the Union were still Lincoln's major war aims; he expressed this belief in his **Gettysburg Address** in 1863— the greatest speech in American history.

Lincoln was reelected in 1864, advocating a reconciliatory policy toward the South after a Union victory. He lived to see the war end on April 9, 1865, but not to implement his plans for Reconstruction. On the night of April 14, 1865, while attending Ford's Theater, a bitter southern sympathizer named **John Wilkes Booth** shot him. Lincoln died the next morning, and he was mourned by millions of Americans.

**Abraham Lincoln**

# 55. Otto von Bismarck
## (1815–1898)

Known as the Iron Chancellor, **Otto Eduard Leopold von Bismarck** united the German states, and for nearly 20 years was "the power behind the throne" of a new **German Empire**.

Bismarck was born in Schonhausen, Prussia (in present-day Germany), into a noble family whose members had been statesmen and soldiers. He studied law at Gottingen and Berlin, and after holding minor judicial and administrative offices, he was elected to the Prussian parliament in 1847. There Bismarck opposed the liberal movement, advocated unification of the various German under the banner of Prussia, and defended the privileges of his elite social class, the Junkers.

During the 1850s, Bismarck was appointed envoy to the Bundestag—the council of German states—and later served as Prussian ambassador to France. In 1862, Emperor **Wilhelm I** named Bismarck chancellor of Prussia. Bismarck's chief aim now was to expel Austria—Prussia's main rival for German supremacy—from the German Confederation, which the two countries agreed to rule jointly. By 1866, friction developed into the **Austro-Prussian War.** Prussia was victorious, and Bismarck formed the North German confederation, from which he excluded Austria.

The desire of French ruler Emperor Napoleon III to expand France's eastern border and incorporate many German states, led in 1870, to the **Franco-Prussian War**, which ended a year later with the defeat of France. Bismarck now easily gathered the German states under the crown of Prussia, with Wilhelm proclaimed kaiser (emperor). Bismarck became the German Empire's first chancellor, a position he held with absolute authority.

To maintain peace for the consolidation of the empire, he advanced a strong military program, gained the friendship of Austria, preserved British neutrality by avoiding naval or colonial rivalry, and isolated France diplomatically to prevent retaliation. With his system of alignments and alliances, Bismarck became the virtual arbiter of Europe.

Bismarck also exerted strong influence upon German domestic affairs. In dealing with the Socialists, Bismarck at first met their opposition with extremely repressive measures. When they once again began to increase their number in parliament, Bismarck instituted a program of sweeping social reform to weaken the socialist platform. His reforms included child labor laws, maximum hours legislation, and extensive old age, illness, and unemployment insurance. His economic policies resulted in the rapid growth of German industry and the acquisition of overseas colonies.

The Bismarck era ended with the accession in 1888 of Emperor **Wilhelm II**. Bismarck soon fell out of favor, and was forced to resign in 1890. He retired to his castle near Hamburg, and spent the remainder of his life criticizing the emperor and his ministers and defending his own policies.

**Otto von Bismarck**

The longest reigning monarch of the British Empire, Queen **Victoria** ruled England at the height of its power both at home and overseas—an era of profound nationalism and conservative morality that came to be called the **Victorian Age.**

Victoria was born at Kensington palace, London, and was the only child of Edward, duke of Kent, the younger brother of King William IV. Her mother was the German princess Mary Louisa Victoria of Saxe-Coburg Gotha. At the age of 18, Victoria emerged from a lonely, secluded childhood to take the throne upon the death of her uncle who died without a male heir.

In 1840, she married her first cousin Prince **Albert**, duke of Saxe-Coburg. Though it was an arranged marriage, it turned out to be a highly romantic and rewarding one. Albert soon became the dominant figure and influence in her life. He encouraged her to exercise her full rights as a constitutional monarch. Victoria and Albert were married for 19 years, and the marriages of their nine children eventually linked the British throne to the royalties of Russia, Germany, Greece, Denmark, and Romania.

Victoria's first prime minister, Lord Melbourne, also had a crucial influence on her. He fostered her self-confidence and enthusiasm for her role, but he also encouraged her to ignore or minimize social problems. Under his influence, she became an ardent **Conservative.**

Victoria's life changed dramatically when Albert died in 1861. In her grief she spent three years in total seclusion; she then continued to wear black and mourn him for the remainder of her life. During the initial period of mourning, when she avoided any public appearances, her popularity declined.

However, she regained the people's admiration when she resumed her determined efforts to steer public affairs. She won particular esteem for fully supporting the popular foreign policies of the Conservative prime minister **Benjamin Disraeli** (see no. 51), who strengthened the power and influence of the Empire during the 1870s. Disraeli also arranged for her to be crowned Empress of India in 1876.

**Queen Victoria**

Conversely, she was continually at odds with **William E. Gladstone**, the Liberal prime minister, whom she intensely disliked, because he favored reforms such as legalizing trade unions and Irish Home Rule.

During the Crimean War (1854–1856), the queen instituted the **Victoria Cross** for bravery, and actively supported the pioneering work of nurse **Florence Nightingale**. By the time she celebrated her diamond jubilee in 1897, her popularity had reached its height, both at home and abroad.

Victoria died at the age of 82 and was buried beside her beloved Albert near Windsor. She was succeeded by her son, Edward VII.

Under the 49-year reign of King **Pedro II**, Brazil achieved great economic and social progress, and saw its prestige and influence rise throughout South America.

Dom Pedro de Alcántara, was born in Rio de Janeiro in 1825. He was the son of Pedro I, the first ruler of an independent Brazil. When he was just five years old, Dom Pedro succeeded to the throne under a regency after his father abdicated. However, the regency was ineffective, and various revolts threatened to divide the huge country into separate states.

To reestablish a direct monarchy, Pedro was declared of age on July 23, 1840 (at the age of 14), and crowned emperor on July 18, 1841. The young ruler quickly used his constitutional power to regulate the groups that wanted to dominate the country.

Pedro II was a calm, serious, and intelligent man, whose reign brought internal peace and economic prosperity to the young nation.

**Pedro II**

Agriculture, commerce, and industry expanded. He diversified the economy—he replaced sugar with coffee as the main export—and cotton farmers, tobacco farmers, ranchers, and rubber extractors were rewarded for their efforts. The government encouraged massive railroad construction—nearly 7,000 miles were completed during Pedro II's reign.

After Pedro had been in power for some ten years, a movement to abolish slavery began to gain strong support. Pedro, who had freed his own slaves in 1840, knew that due to the power of the landed aristocracy, slavery would have to be phased out gradually. In 1850, he signed the **Queiroz Law**, pledging Brazil's navy to join the international effort to stamp out the Atlantic slave trade. In 1871, the Rio Branco Law—the **Law of Free Birth**—took effect. It stated that children born to slaves after that year were to be freed after a certain number of years in servitude. In 1888, complete emancipation was decreed; 700,000 slaves were freed, with no compensation for the owners.

In foreign affairs, Brazil extended its influence west and southwest throughout the continent. It helped overthrow the Argentine dictator Manuel de Rosas, and conducted a major war against Paraguay, in alliance with Uruguay and Argentina.

By 1870, a movement toward a republican form of government began to spread in Brazil. Pedro II began to lose support within the military and the aristocracy. In the meantime, the emperor's objections to certain laws passed by the Roman Catholic Church strained relations with the clergy.

With these powerful forces allied against him, his downfall seemed inevitable. On November 15, 1889, a military coup forced Pedro II to abdicate. He went into exile in Europe and died in Paris in 1891.

# 58. Georges Clémenceau
## (1841–1929)

As prime minister of France, **Georges Clémenceau** was a driving force in the Allied victory in **World War I**.

Clémenceau was born in Mouilleron-en-Pareds, on the west coast of France. As a young man, he went to Paris to study medicine, but his republican politics brought him in conflict with the government of Napoleon III. In 1865, he went to the United States, where he worked as a journalist and teacher.

Clémenceau then returned to France to practice medicine. After the government of Napoleon III was ousted in 1870, the Third Republic was declared. In 1876, Clémenceau was elected to the **Chamber of Deputies**, quickly becoming a leader of the Radical party. A passionate, aggressive critic, Clémenceau soon earned the nickname, **"The Tiger."**

In 1880, he started his newspaper, *La Justice*. His reputation as a political critic grew. However, in 1892, he was linked to a scandal involving the Panama Canal, and the following year he lost his bid for reelection.

During the next nine years, he established another daily newspaper, *L'Aurore*. It was through this paper that Clémenceau championed the cause of **Alfred Dreyfus**, a Jewish army captain accused of treason. Clémenceau's staunch support of Dreyfus brought him back into favor with his fellow republicans. Clémenceau was elected to the Senate in 1902 and became premier in 1906. During his tenure, he carried out many social reforms, quelled workers' strikes, and carried out the measure separating church and state. In 1909, he lost the premiership to **Aristide Briand**.

Through his newspapers and public speeches, Clémenceau had long urged preparation for war, which he believed was coming. When the war broke out, he became an outspoken opponent of **Joseph Joffre**, chief of the general staff of the

**Georges Clémenceau**

French Army.

By 1917, the war had dragged on for three years; it had cost France millions of lives, and millions of dollars in property damage. In November, French President Raymond Poincaré appointed Clémenceau prime minister. Immediately, he began rallying the dispirited French people. He helped persuade the Allies to accept a unified command under the French marshal, General **Ferdinand Foch**. With the addition of U.S. forces, the Allies swept to victory over Germany within a year.

Clémenceau presided over the **Paris Peace Conference** in 1919, and he and U.S. President **Woodrow Wilson** were the major architects of the treaty. However, while Clémenceau managed to restore Alsace-Lorraine to France, the other delegates would not agree with his further demands, which included extremely harsh terms against Germany. The following year, Clémenceau was defeated in an election for president by **Paul Deschanel**. He retired from politics and wrote his memoirs, *The Grandeur and Misery of Victory*. Clémenceau died in Paris in 1929.

# 59. Mutsuhito (Meiji)
## (1852–1912)

Under the Meiji Emperor **Mutsuhito** Japan was dramatically transformed from a feudal society to a centralized, modern industrial and military power.

The second son of Emperor Komei, Mutsuhito was born in Kyoto in 1852, and was declared crown prince—heir to the throne—in 1860. His education was considered liberal, though he was trained with discipline and rigor, both athletically and intellectually. After his father died in 1867, Mutsuhito ascended the throne, taking the name Meiji, by which the era of his reign is also known. The beginning of his rule coincided with the end of the *shogunate*, the more than 650-year dictatorial rule of Japan by warrior families, and the restoration to the emperor of supreme executive authority in the country.

Unlike his father, the young emperor agreed with the growing popular consensus on the need for modernizing Japan along Western lines. This idea had developed as a result of the country's recent contact with other nations through trade, after a 250-year period of cultural and economic isolation. At his January 1868 coronation, Meiji took the "**Charter Oath of Five Principles**," promising a course of Westernization in government. A year later, he moved the capital from the remote city of Kyoto to the more commercial city of Edo (renamed Tokyo).

Between 1871 and 1890, the emperor formally ordered the abolition of the feudal system, the establishment of a new school system, adoption of the cabinet system of government, the introduction of a parliament (the Diet), and promulgation of a Western-style constitution. In addition, he ordered imported machines and tools from advanced Western nations.

As a result of the new constitution, the emperor's political role became largely ceremonial—relegated to opening the Diet, holding ministerial meetings, and issuing proclamations. Nevertheless, Meiji was not a passive observer of the changes. He made carefully orchestrated public appearance, that along with his disciplined and frugal lifestyle, endeared him to the people.

Meiji did, however, play an active role as commander-in-chief in the **Sino-Japanese War** (1894–1895), fought over control of Korea. In this war, which the Japanese easily dominated and which resulted in an independent Korea, Japan showed just how much it had adapted Western military techniques and technology.

Then in the **Russo-Japanese War** (1904–1905), Meiji oversaw policy. However, heavy casualties and a less than satisfactory peace settlement triggered social unrest, which the emperor tried to appease by increasing assistance to the needy and advancing social causes.

By the end of Meiji's reign, the role of the emperor had become closer to that of a deity—above the mundane concerns of practical governance. Mutsuhito died in 1912, and was succeeded by his son, Yoshihito.

**Mutsuhito**

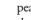

# 60. Woodrow Wilson
## (1856–1924)

A scholar turned politician, **Woodrow Wilson** brought high-minded idealism to the presidency, and then was forced to lead his country through the first of the 20th century's world wars.

Born in Virginia in 1856, Wilson was the son of a Presbyterian minister. After graduating college, he studied law, government and history, before becoming a professor and scholar. In 1902, he became president of **Princeton University** in New Jersey, where he instituted many reforms.

He entered politics in 1910, when the **Democratic party** backed him in a successful bid for governor of New Jersey. Buoyed by his sweeping reform program as governor, he captured the 1912 Democratic presidential nomination. When Theodore Roosevelt's third-party bid split the Republican opposition, Wilson took the presidency with 41 percent of the popular vote.

Wilson brought the progressive agenda he had promoted in New Jersey to Washington. During his first three years in office, he initiated programs that provided federal oversight of banking and Wall Street (the **Federal Reserve System**), the graduated income tax, support of labor organizations, and federal aid to education and agriculture.

In foreign affairs Wilson sought to keep the United States out of Europe's troubles. He viewed the outbreak of war in 1914 as the result of European imperialistic rivalries, and sought to protect American neutrality in the face of violations of American rights on the high seas.

Reelected in a close election in 1916, Wilson met with triumph and tragedy during his second term. His efforts to end the war through mediation failed, and in April 1917, he asked Congress to declare war against Germany in response to U-boat attacks on American shipping. The tide of the war turned in favor of the Allies, and Germany sued for peace in 1918. Wilson attended the **Paris Peace Conference** in 1919, and was hailed by enthusiastic crowds in France. While he helped hammer out the **Treaty of Versailles**, he was forced to yield on many points to the leaders of France and Great Britain.

Exhausted and ailing, Wilson returned home to face the biggest fight of his career—obtaining Senate approval of the treaty and America's entry into the **League of Nations**. The strain of fighting Republican isolationist senators proved too much for him. On October 2, 1919, Wilson suffered a massive stroke that left him partially paralyzed on his left side. His wife, Edith, controlled access to him, made decisions by default, and engineered a cover-up of his condition for the rest of his term. Though the Senate rejected the treaty, Wilson never wavered in his dream that the United States should join the League of Nations. He died in his sleep at his Washington home in 1924.

**Woodrow Wilson**

# 61. David Lloyd George
## (1863–1945)

Statesman, reformer, and prime minister, Great Britain's **David Lloyd George** led his country to victory in **World War I**.

A native of Manchester, Lloyd George was the son of a Welsh elementary school headmaster. His father died when he was one year old, and he was sent to Wales to be raised by his uncle. As a young man he studied law, and soon became known as a defender of the people against those in authority. In 1888, he married Margaret Owens, and they would eventually have five children.

**(left to right) Lloyd George, Georges Clémenceau, and Woodrow Wilson**

In 1890, Lloyd George was elected to the **House of Commons** as a Liberal representing a district in Wales; at age 27, he was the youngest member of the chamber. By the turn of the century he had gained a reputation for spirited oratory on behalf of Welsh causes. He established himself as Liberal leader, and was an outspoken opponent of the second Boer War (1899–1902).

In 1908, under Prime Minister Herbert Asquith, Lloyd George became **chancellor of the Exchequer**. He introduced and fought for

the passage of bills for old-age pensions (1908) and national insurance (1911). In 1914, after the outbreak of World War I, his job was to secure the largest war loans in British history, and to stabilize credit to meet the war's demands.

In December 1916, Prime Minister Asquith and his cabinet resigned, having lost the confidence of the country over the handling of the war. Lloyd George then became prime minister and took firm control of the government.

Lloyd George proved a capable, aggressive wartime leader, and the victory achieved in 1918 was won despite conflicts with the commander-in-chief of the British Expeditionary Forces. At the war's end, Lloyd George was instrumental in negotiating the **Treaty of Versailles**, and helped forge compromise among the different parties.

After the 1918 British general election, Lloyd George served as prime minister in a coalition government with Liberals and Conservatives. During the campaign, he had promised comprehensive reforms to deal with education, housing, health, and transportation. The Conservative party, however, had no desire to introduce these reforms. Lloyd George lost further Conservative support when he sponsored the **Home Rule Bill** in 1920, and was largely instrumental in the establishment of an **Irish Free State** in 1921. In October that year, the Conservatives withdrew their support for the government, and Lloyd George resigned. He was reelected to Parliament, and remained the leader of the Liberal party.

Throughout the 1920s and 1930s, Lloyd George continued to campaign for progressive causes, although he remained in semiretirement for a number of years until his death in March 1945.

The most prominent Greek politician and statesman of the early 20th century, **Eleutherios Venizélos** led a nationalist movement against the **Ottoman Turks** and spent years trying to turn **Greece** away from a monarchy and into a republic.

Born on the island of Crete—then a part of the Ottoman Empire—Venizélos spent part of his young life in Athens; his family lived there after Turkey expelled them from Crete because of his father's role in an anti-Turk rebellion. While in Athens, Venizélos became a Greek citizen and later studied law there.

After he returned to Crete, Venizélos became a member of the **National Assembly**, heading the newly formed **Liberal party**. In 1905, and then again in 1908, as leader of the assembly, Venizélos declared Cretan unison with Greece. However, in both instances, Athens would not officially accept this move.

In January 1910, rebels launched a coup against the Athenian government. Venizélos was invited to Athens, and in October he became **prime minister** of Greece. He immediately began a program of reform in civil service and education. Venizélos also reorganized the armed forces, and in the Balkan wars of 1912–1913, helped rid the Balkan peninsula of the Ottoman Empire. In the war's aftermath, Greece doubled its territory and population, acquiring southern Macedonia, southern Ípiros, Crete, and some of the Aegean Islands.

At the outbreak of **World War I**, Venizélos wanted Greece to join the Allies, but was opposed by Greece's pro-German king, Constantine I. Because of the king's opposition, Venizélos resigned as prime minister in 1915. For two years, the Allies pressured Greece to cease its pro-German activities. In June 1917, the Allies forced Constantine into exile, Venizélos became prime minister again, and Greece entered the war on the Allied side.

When hostilities ended, Venizélos participated in the peace conferences in Paris.

In 1920, Venizélos led Greece in an invasion of Turkey. However, the campaign proved to be a disaster. Later that year the Greek people voted for a coalition of monarchist parties, and King Constantine was recalled. Venizélos abruptly resigned and exiled himself in Paris.

**Eleutherios Venizélos**

Over the next several years, the Greek government alternated between periods of monarchy and republic. During this time, Venizélos served as prime minister twice (1924, 1928–1932). In the general election of 1928, he won a majority, and formed his third and last cabinet. During his tenure, he restored normal relations with all of Greece's Balkan neighbors.

The effects of the Great Depression in the early 1930s weakened Venizélos's domestic position and he met with defeat in the elections of 1932. His political career ended in 1935 and he left for Paris, where he died the next year.

# 63. Sun Yat-sen
## (1866–1925)

Known as the father of modern China, **Sun Yat-sen** founded the Chinese nationalist movement and served as the first provisional president of the **Republic of China**.

Sun Yat-sen was born at Hsiang-shan, Kwangtung province, the son of a peasant. When he was 13 years-old, he went to Hawaii to attend an English missionary school where he came under Western influences. He later went on to study medicine in Canton and in Hong Kong, where he graduated in 1892.

Committed to Westernizing China, Sun turned to politics in 1894. Forsaking his medical practice, he traveled north that year and joined revolutionaries trying to overthrow the **Manchu** dynasty and establish a republic. When the revolt failed, he fled the country, living as an exile from 1895 to 1911.

Sun then traveled to the United States and Great Britain, studying Western political and social theory. He soon began to gain widespread publicity and support for his Chinese nationalist movement. In 1907, he issued his three great principles—nationalism, democracy, and people's livelihood—a socialism that would provide food, shelter, and clothing for all people.

In 1911, Sun returned to China during the revolution that overthrew the Manchu dynasty. He was then elected provisional president of the Chinese republic. At the same time, China had broken into regions that military warlords ruled, and Sun was later forced to resign in favor of **Yüan Shih-kai**, who had taken over the north of China. Sun opposed Yüan's dictatorial methods and organized an unsuccessful revolt. Once again he fled, this time to Japan.

When Yüan died in 1916, Sun returned to China and in 1921 was elected president of the Southern Chinese Republic. Meanwhile, because he could not obtain aid from either the West or Japan, he looked to the new government of the **Soviet Union** to help him in his quest to stabilize all of China.

In 1924, to hasten the conquest of China, he began a policy of active cooperation with the **Chinese Communists**, and accepted the help of the USSR in reorganizing the Chinese Nationalist party (the **Kuomintang**). It was transformed into a tightly disciplined body with authority descending from the top to the lower levels, on the model of the Soviet Communist party. With a strong party and a strong army, Sun planned to march north and seize the capital.

It was not to be—he died of cancer in Peking in March 1925. After his death, the Communists, led by Mao Tse-tung, and the Kuomintang, led by Chiang Kai-shek split, with each group claiming to be his true heir. The two groups would wage a protracted war for control of China until the Communists emerged victorious in 1949.

**Sun Yat-sen**

70

# 64. Nicholas II
## (1868–1918)

With a tragic combination of cruel fate and misguided policies, the 300-year-old **Russian Romanov** dynasty came crashing down during the reign of **Nicholas II**.

Born in 1868, Nicholas was the eldest son of Czar Alexander III and princess Dagmar of Denmark. In 1889, Nicholas became very attracted to his distant cousin, Alix of Hesse, a granddaughter of Britain's Queen Victoria.

The couple were to be married in 1894, when Czar Alexander died suddenly, and Nicholas succeeded to the throne. The wedding took place one week after the funeral; prior to the marriage, Alix converted to the Russian Orthodox faith, and changed her name to **Alexandra**. Over the next ten years, the couple had four daughters, and then in 1904, Alexandra gave birth to a son, Alexis. It was soon discovered that the boy was afflicted with hemophilia, a life-threatening bleeding disease.

As he himself admitted, Nicholas was not by temperament prepared to undertake the complex tasks of ruler. However, he dreamed of expanding his empire, particularly in Korea, where Japan already had a foothold. Instead, Russia's humiliating defeats in the **Russo-Japanese War** (1904–1905) fomented the growing discontent at home. A revolution broke out in 1905, bringing strikes, terrorism, and peasant violence suppressed by military force.

By 1912, support for the monarchy was wavering. Russia's entry into **World War I** in 1914 made matters worse. With an ill-equipped, poorly-trained, and badly-led army, the action was a disaster.

Nicholas personally assumed command of the army, and in his absence, the empress exerted great influence on the government. She also turned more and more to **Rasputin**, an unsavory self-professed faith healer, who she believed could cure her son of his life-threatening disease. Worthless nominees of Rasputin replaced competent ministers and officials. Treachery ran rampant, until finally, Rasputin's enemies murdered him.

When food riots and workers' strikes broke out in the capital on March 8, 1917, troops were sent to restore order. Instead, they refused to fire on their countrymen, and many joined the revolt. Four days later, the government resigned and the emperor was called on to abdicate. On March 15, 1917, Nicholas abdicated in favor of his brother Michael, who refused the crown. The royal family was then detained at their palace at Tsarskoye Selo.

In November, 1917, **Vladimir Lenin** (see no. 66) and the Bolsheviks seized power. In April 1918, the royal family was taken to **Ekaterinburg** in the Ural Mountains. In the early morning of July 17, a Bolshevik firing squad executed the czar, his wife and their children; their bodies were cast into an abandoned mineshaft and burned. The Romanov dynasty had come to a violent and tragic end.

**Nicholas II being guarded
by Bolshevik forces**

# 65. Neville Chamberlain
## (1869–1940)

Remembered as the architect of an appeasement policy towards Nazi Germany that was an utter failure, **Neville Chamberlain** was the British prime minister at the outbreak of World War II.

The son of Joseph Chamberlain, well-known mayor of Birmingham, the young Chamberlain was educated at Rugby School. After a successful career in the copper-brass business, he followed his father's path and became active in politics. In 1918, he was elected to parliament as a **Conservative**.

During the 1920s, Chamberlain served as health minister under Prime Minister Stanley Baldwin. In that position, Chamberlain introduced a series of important social reforms in the areas of housing, pensions, and insurance. From 1931 to 1937, Chamberlain served as chancellor of the Exchequer under Baldwin. When Baldwin resigned in 1937, Chamber-lain became prime minister in a coalition gov-ernment formed to deal with Britain's eco-nomic troubles.

**Neville Chamberlain**

Chamberlain soon had other problems. Under Adolf Hitler, Nazi Germany was rearming and making aggressive advances along its southern and eastern borders. Chamberlain was desperate to avoid a European war, at least until Great Britain could prepare itself better economically and militarily. In a futile attempt to sway fascist Italy away from German influence, he agreed to recognize Italian supremacy in Ethiopia. He also stood aside while Germany occupied and then annexed Austria in 1938.

Then when Hitler demanded that Czechoslovakia cede the **Sudentenland**—an area in Czechoslovakia where many Germans lived—to Germany, Chamberlain met person-ally with Hitler and signed the **Munich Agreement** in September 1938. In this pact, he and French Premier **Edouard Daladier** granted Hitler almost all of his demands in regard to Czechoslovakia. The Munich Agreement became a symbol of appeasement and shook the confidence of Eastern Europeans in the good faith of the Western democracies.

When Hitler invaded Czechoslovakia, Chamberlain reversed his appeasement policy and soon proclaimed Anglo-French guarantees of armed support for Poland, Romania, and Greece in the event of similar attacks. After the German attack on Poland on September 1, 1939, Chamberlain coun-tered with a British declara-tion of war two days later. He remained prime minis-ter during the initial period of sporadic military action. At this time, Winston Churchill was brought into his cabi-net as first lord of the Admiralty.

After Norway fell to the Germans in April 1940, Chamberlain lost the support of many members of the Labor party and Liberal party, and he was forced to resign on May 10, 1940. **Winston Churchill** became prime minis-ter in a coalition government of Conservatives and Laborites. Chamberlain served briefly in his cabinet until October, 1940, when ill health forced him to resign. He died the fol-lowing month in Heckfield, near Reading, Hampshire.

# 66. Vladimir Lenin
## (1870–1924)

**Vladimir Lenin** was the leader of the Bolshevik Revolution in Russia, and the architect, builder, and head of the world's first communist state—the **Soviet Union**.

Vladimir Ilich Ulyanov (he later changed his name to Lenin), was born in Western Russia, the son of a schoolmaster. In 1887, Vladimir's eldest brother was hanged for his role in a plot to assassinate Czar Alexander III. This unquestionably influenced Lenin's subsequent decision to take the path of revolution.

Lenin studied law at the universities of Kazan and St. Petersburg, and graduated in 1891. He immersed himself in the teachings of **Karl Marx**, became a Marxist and began revolutionary activities in St. Petersburg. He was arrested in 1895, and exiled to Siberia; when his exile ended in 1900, he left Russia to continue his revolutionary activities abroad.

In 1902, while in London, Lenin became leader of the **Bolsheviks**, the minority faction of Russia's Social Democratic Workers' party. While he was abroad, Lenin published many pamphlets and socialist studies, and founded two socialist newspapers. A fiery speaker who was fluent in several languages, Lenin became the acknowledged leader of the movement to overthrow the monarchy in Russia.

In March 1917, Lenin was smuggled back into Russia with the help of Germany, which knew that his position was to remove Russia from **World War I** and sue for peace. In October, the provisional government that had replaced the czar was on the verge of collapsing. Using the strength they had established in the "soviets," the unions of workers that had formed in St. Petersburg, Moscow, and elsewhere, Lenin and the Bolsheviks seized the reigns of power.

The new government's first acts were to propose an armistice with Germany, and to abolish private ownership of land and distribute it among the peasants. Banks were nationalized and workers' control over factory production was introduced. The Cheka, or political police, ruthlessly suppressed all opposition. The Bolsheviks then became the **Communist** party.

By late 1918, the Communists' power was being threatened by forces from Western nations and the pro-monarchist White Army looking to restore the czar. A civil war raged until late 1920, when the Communist Red Army triumphed. In 1922, the Communists brought together all the territories they controlled and organized them into one federation called the Union of Soviet Socialist Republics (USSR).

With communism proving inadequate to put the country on its feet, Lenin introduced the **New Economic Policy** (NEP) in 1921 that allowed some private enterprise. Before he could see it fully implemented, however, Lenin fell seriously ill in the spring of 1922. He suffered a series of strokes over the next two years and died on January 21, 1924.

**Vladimir Lenin**

Undoubtedly one of the greatest public figures of the 20th century, **Winston Churchill** rallied the British people during **World War II** and as prime minister, led his country from the brink of defeat to victory.

Born at Oxfordshire, England, he was the eldest son of Lord Randolph Churchill and Jennie Jerome, a wealthy American. When he was 21, Churchill joined the army and served in India, Egypt, and South Africa. He entered politics in 1900s, winning election to the House of Commons as a **Conservative**. He remained a member of Parliament, almost without interruption, for 60 years.

During the 1920s and 1930s, Churchill wrote and remained in the public eye with his support for Edward VIII in the abdication crisis of 1936, and with his vehement opposition to the Indian nationalist movement. He also issued unheeded warnings of the threat from Nazi Germany.

**President Roosevelt and Winston Churchill at their meeting in 1941**

When World War II broke out in September 1939, Neville Chamberlain appointed him first lord of the admiralty. In May 1940, Chamberlain resigned, and Churchill became both prime minister and defense minister at the head of a coalition government. Using his great oratorical skills, boundless energy, and courageous optimism in the face of the relentless German war machine, Churchill rallied the British people during the grim years from 1940 to 1942 and helped save Europe from total Nazi domination.

Churchill developed a close relationship with U.S. president **Franklin D. Roosevelt** (see no. 71), and in August 1941, the two leaders concluded the **Atlantic Charter**, a statement of democratic principles that dealt with among other things, territorial rights and self-government. During the war, the two men were responsible for developing the overall strategy for retaking Europe from the German occupation. In 1945, Churchill met with Roosevelt and Soviet leader **Josef Stalin** at the Yalta Conference to draw plans for the final defeat of Germany, and for its occupation and control after its unconditional surrender.

In July 1945, Churchill lost his bid for reelection after Britain's desire for rapid social reform led to a Labor victory. In 1946, on a visit to the United States, Churchill made a controversial speech at Fulton, Missouri, in which he prophetically warned of the expansive tendencies of the Soviet Union and coined the expression "**Iron Curtain.**"

Churchill again became prime minister in 1951 and served four years before resigning because of ill health. In 1953 he was knighted and awarded the Nobel Prize in Literature for his numerous historical writings. While his peacetime government saw a revival in the country's economy, there was, however, little progress toward the united Europe which Churchill favored. He died on January 24, 1965, in London.

# 68. Josef Stalin
## (1879–1953)

As the leader of the Soviet Union for nearly 50 years, **Josef Stalin** industrialized and transformed the country into a world power. However, the Soviet people paid a high price for his official policies and personal paranoia—under his iron fist, millions of innocent people were imprisoned and killed.

He was born Josef Vissarionovich Dzhugashvili (he later changed his name to Stalin), in Georgia, a Russian colony in the Caucasus. As a young man, Stalin studied for the priesthood, but was expelled from the seminary for his leftist politics. He then became a **Marxist** and joined the Social Democratic party. After the party split into two factions, Menshevik and Bolshevik, in 1903, Stalin joined the **Bolsheviks** and became a disciple of their leader, **Vladimir Lenin** (see no. 66).

Stalin played only a modest role in the Bolshevik Revolution of 1917. However, after Lenin died in 1924, he outmaneuvered his main rivals, including **Leon Trotsky**, and gained control of the Communist party. Over the next few years, he launched a series of five-year plans to collectivize industry and agriculture. Stalin maintained that his program of consolidating "socialism in one country," although demanding immense sacrifice and discipline, would render the Soviet Union immune to attacks by outside capitalist nations.

To accomplish these goals, however, Stalin used repressive measures and terror. The kulaks, farmers who had risen to prosperity, were shot, exiled, or absorbed into the rapidly expanding network of concentration camps (*gulags*) and worked to death. During the 1930s, Stalin orchestrated purges of top Communist party and Russian army officials, to eliminate any threats to his total control of the nation. Thousands of people, were shot or sent to the gulags, where they either perished or remained for decades.

Stalin signed a nonaggression pact with Germany in 1939, which was designed to forestall **Adolf Hitler's** desire to conquer both western and eastern Europe. Ultimately, Germany violated the pact and invaded the Soviet Union on June 22, 1941. Stalin took over the directions of military operations and joined forces with the Western allies. The Soviet army fought valiantly on the Eastern front, driving the Nazis back toward Germany. This enabled Stalin to demand many concessions from Great Britain and the United States at both the **Yalta** and **Potsdam** conferences, allowing him to establish Soviet dominance in Eastern Europe after the war.

Because of declining health and his paranoia, Stalin made few public appearances in the late 1940s and early 1950s. His remoteness only stimulated the public worship bestowed on him and created a cult following. He increased repression and persecution of his closest collaborators in his later years, reminiscent of the purges of the 1930s.

Stalin died of a cerebral hemorrhage on March 5, 1953.

**Josef Stalin**

# 69. Mustapha Kemal Atatürk
## (1881–1938)

**Mustapha Kemal Atatürk**

The first president of the Republic of Turkey, **Mustapha Kemal** was a soldier, statesman, and reformer who was not above being a ruthless dictator to accomplish his goal of modernizing his nation.

He was born in Salonika, in northern Greece, then a Muslim Ottoman province. In 1902, he graduated from a Turkish military academy in Constantinople (present-day Istanbul), and advanced through the ranks of the Turkish army, seeing action in both the Balkan War (1912–1913) and World War I (1914–1918).

In the aftermath of World War I, Turkey, which fought on the side of the Central Powers, was divided under British and Greek rule. Violently opposed to this, Kemal resigned from the army and joined activists desiring sovereignty for Turkey. After the sultan outlawed him, he set up a rival government at Ankara, in 1921, and became the symbol of Turkish nationalism. His forces drove the Greeks from Anatolia, in central Turkey, the Greek civilians being left to the mercies of the Turkish army and vengeful Turkish population.

In 1922, Kemal's government reached a peace agreement with Great Britain; in short order, the Ottoman sultan was deposed and Turkey was declared a self-governing republic. Kemal was elected president in 1923 and later reelected in 1927, 1931, and 1935 by a unanimous parliament.

He immediately began a program of sweeping social and political reform, including a vigorous campaign for modernization. Women were raised to legal equality with men. They were also given the right to vote and permitted to sit in the assembly. In Kemal's quest to secularize Turkey, Islam ceased to be the state religion. Civil marriages were made compulsory, men could not wear the fez of Muslim dress, and women were strongly discouraged from wearing the veil.

Among Kemal's other reforms were the use of the Latin alphabet to replace Arabic script and better educational opportunities. In 1934, he instituted a five-year plan for the development of industry, and the government encouraged agriculture, the opening of mines, and railroad and road construction.

By 1935, surnames, long used in the West, were now required of all people. Kemal took the name of **Atatürk**, meaning "**Father of the Turks**." When devout Muslims and ethnic minorities such as the Kurds and Armenians opposed his tactics, he retaliated with martial law and the ruthless use of the army.

In foreign affairs, Kemal pursued a policy of conciliation and neutrality. He signed a peace treaty with Greece, a naval agreement with Russia, and settled a frontier dispute with Persia.

While his rule often resembled a dictatorship, at the time of his death in 1938, Kemal had succeeded in bringing Turkey into the 20th century.

# 70. Angelo Roncalli (Pope John XXIII)
## (1881–1963)

Although his papal reign was brief, Pope **John XXIII** transformed the **Roman Catholic Church** during the latter half of the 20th century.

He was born **Angelo Roncalli**, to a poor farming family near Bergamo, in northern Italy. An intelligent and gifted boy, he was sent to seminary schools to prepare for the priesthood before he was ten years old. He was ordained in 1904, and began a steady climb through church ranks. Roncalli served as a sergeant in the Italian medical corps during **World War I**. This experience broadened his view of life; he would be one of the few popes who had witnessed human suffering on a large scale and in a first-hand manner.

Roncalli became a monsignor in 1921, and was raised to archbishop in 1925. He was then sent on a number of prestigious diplomatic assignments. He spent nearly 20 years in the Eastern Mediterranean, and during World War II, he played an important role in rescuing Jews in Hungary, Bulgaria, and Turkey.

In 1944, he was appointed *papal nuncio* (highest-ranking papal representative) to the newly liberated Paris, and he used his diplomatic skills to reconcile clergy and Catholic citizens who had resisted the Nazis with those who had collaborated. In 1953, he became a cardinal and served as patriarch of Venice.

Pope Pius XII died in 1958, and although the 77-year-old Roncalli had achieved great stature within the Church, there was still great surprise when was elected pope.

Pope John surprised many people himself by summoning a **Vatican Council**, a meeting of 3,000 of the world's Catholic bishops, as well as lay Catholics. The Council's task was to bring the Church, which had lost touch with the political, scientific, and technological changes of the past 100 years, up-to-date and reinvigorate its reputation. In October, 1962, John XXIII presided over the Council's first session himself. As a great reconciler, he cordially received Eastern Orthodox, Anglican, and Protestant religious leaders, inviting them to send observers to the Council.

Pope John also embarked upon a new start toward **Christian unity**—to lay aside past hostilities and acknowledge Catholics' share of the responsibility for a divided Christianity. He sent representatives to the 1961 **World Council of Churches** in New Delhi, India, whereas earlier popes had spurned this organization; he also named the first Indian and African cardinals.

Pope John's greatest claim to world affection, however, rested on his warm personality; extremely open, he mingled freely with his flock, visiting prisons and schools, and meeting with diverse groups, many of whom were non-Catholics. At his death in 1963, he was one the best loved men in the world, admired by Catholics and non-Catholics alike.

**Pope John XXIII**

The most influential U.S. president of the 20th century, **Franklin D. Roosevelt** served as his nation's leader during one of the most turbulent periods of American history—the **Great Depression** and **World War II**.

Franklin Delano Roosevelt was born into a wealthy Anglo–Dutch-American family in Hyde Park, New York. In 1905, he married his distant cousin, **Eleanor Roosevelt**. He entered politics in 1911 when he was elected New York state senator. He then went on to become assistant secretary of the Navy (1913–1920), and ran unsuccessfully as the **Democratic** candidate for vice president in 1920. The following year tragedy struck—he contracted polio, a crippling disease that left him paralyzed from the waist down. However, he overcame his handicap, and in 1928 was elected governor of New York; he was reelected in 1930.

Then, in 1932, a desperate nation, deeply mired in the Great Depression, overwhelmingly elected Roosevelt president. Over the next four years, he introduced several new programs to try to restore the U.S. economy. He spoke often to the nation in his "fireside chats," and his confident, optimistic demeanor in the face of America's darkest economic period helped give the people hope. Many of the administration's programs eased the crisis, and in 1936, Roosevelt was overwhelmingly reelected to a second term.

Soon after World War II broke out in 1939, Roosevelt, fearful that America would eventually be drawn into the conflict, launched a vast rearmament program; he also instituted policies that would supply armaments to the European Allies.

In the summer of 1940, after France fell and while the Germans were bombing Great Britain, Roosevelt increased aid to the Allies. With war looming closer to home, Roosevelt broke a long-standing precedent in running for a third term. The country had such confidence in his leadership that once again he was easily reelected.

On December 7, 1941, the Japanese attack on **Pearl Harbor** plunged the United States into the war. Now Roosevelt took the lead in establishing a grand alliance among all the countries fighting the Axis powers. Along with Winston Churchill and Josef Stalin, Roosevelt developed the overall strategy the Allies used to win the war.

In 1944, with the ultimate Allied victory in sight, Roosevelt ran for a fourth term as president, and once again was easily reelected. In early 1945, Roosevelt met Churchill and Stalin at the Yalta Conference to plan the political framework for the postwar world. On April 12, 1945, about a month before Germany surrendered to the Allies, Roosevelt died suddenly from a cerebral hemorrhage at the "Little White House" in Warm Springs, Georgia. Millions of people, at home and abroad, mourned his death.

**Franklin D. Roosevelt**

# Benito Mussolini
## (1883–1945)

**Benito Mussolini** came to power in Italy during the 1920s promising to restore the glory of the Roman Empire. Instead he led his country into a disastrous alliance with **Nazi Germany** that brought it destruction and humiliating defeat in **World War II**.

Mussolini was born in 1883 in Predappio, in northern Italy, the son of a blacksmith. In 1902, he immigrated to Switzerland, where he was imprisoned more than once for inciting violence during trade union strikes. After returning to Italy, Mussolini became active in the Socialist party, but he was expelled from the party in 1914 because he was in favor of Italy entering World War I.

In 1919, he formed a new political party— a fascist movement that was anti-socialist, anti-Communist, but also anti-capitalist. Called the **Blackshirts**, because of their military style outfits, Mussolini's group promised to solve Italy's economic problems with a strong central government based in Rome.

In October, 1922, Mussolini led a massive **March on Rome**, backed by thousands of supporters. Faced with Mussolini's growing strength and popularity, the king appointed him prime minister.

Mussolini quickly moved to take full control of the government. The parliamentary system was virtually abolished, law codes were rewritten, and he personally chose newspaper editors. Those who resisted him were treated ruthlessly. He won the cooperation of his financial backers by transferring a number of industries from public to private ownership. At the same time, he improved conditions for working people, and created many public works projects.

By the 1930s, Mussolini began to concentrate on foreign policy, trying to restore Italy to the days of the Roman Empire through conquest. His forces conquered **Albania** and **Ethiopia**, and beginning in 1936, Mussolini

**Benito Mussolini**

formed close ties with Germany and its Nazi leader, **Adolf Hitler**.

Mussolini's armed forces were completely unprepared when Hitler's invasion of Poland in 1939 led to the outbreak of World War II. Mussolini decided to remain "nonbelligerent" until he felt certain which side would win. Only after the fall of France in June 1940 did he declare war on the Allies. In 1941, he followed Hitler in declaring war on the United States.

Following Italian defeats on all fronts and the Anglo-American landing in Sicily in 1943, most of Mussolini's colleagues turned against him, and he was arrested. Rescued by the Germans several months later, he set up a Republican Fascist state in northern Italy, but he was little more than a puppet of the German army. Increasingly, he tried to shift the blame for defeat onto the Italian people.

In April 1945, just before the Allied armies reached Milan, Mussolini, along with his mistress Clara Petacci, were caught by Italian partisans and executed.

# 73. David Ben-Gurion
## (1886–1973)

A Zionist statesman and political leader, **David Ben-Gurion** became the first prime minister of the newly formed nation of **Israel**.

Born in Plonsk, Poland, Ben-Gurion received a traditional Jewish education; as a young man he became interested in **Zionism**, the late 19th century worldwide movement for the establishment of an official Jewish state in **Palestine**. Between 1904 and 1906, he worked as a teacher in Warsaw and was involved in Labor Zionist politics. In 1906, he immigrated to Palestine—at the time, part of the Ottoman Empire. During World War I, Ben-Gurion fought with the English against the Turks. After the war, he returned to Palestine, which was now under English rule, and became active in the Zionist movement.

In 1921, Ben-Gurion became secretary-general of the Jewish Labor Federation. In 1930, he was elected leader of the **Mapai party**, the socialist faction within the World Zionist Organization.

Ben-Gurion helped lead the struggle for the creation of a Jewish state. His program of **Zionist Socialism** described the economic, industrial, agricultural, educational, military, and cultural infrastructure on which the future Jewish state would be built.

While calling for a strong Jewish defense force, Ben-Gurion also realized the need to maintain working relations with the British government as long as the Jewish community in Palestine was small and relatively weak. The situation worsened in May 1939 when the British limited Jewish immigration to Palestine and all but banned the sale of land to Jews there.

In 1945, Ben-Gurion visited the **Holocaust** survivors in camps in Germany and became convinced of the absolute necessity of the immediate establishment of the Jewish state. He pushed for an activist anti-British policy of resistance and began to prepare the underground army, the Haganah, for the coming inevitable struggle for independence.

In 1947, the British turned the entire Palestine question over to the United Nations, and in 1948, the U. N. voted to partition Palestine into one Arab state, and one Jewish state. Ben-Gurion then proclaimed the birth of the nation of Israel in May 1948.

Ben-Gurion became Israel's first prime minister and minister for defense, serving in those positions until 1953, and then after a two-year absence, serving again from 1958–1963. During this critical period, Israel fought and won several small wars against its Arab neighbors, received and absorbed over a million immigrants, developed its economy, and forged its diplomatic position in the world.

Ben-Gurion retired in 1963, but came back to politics two years later to lead a new coalition of Labor party members who favored a more "hawkish" strategy in dealing with Israel's Arab enemies. In 1970 Ben-Gurion retired for good from all political activity. He died in 1973.

**David Ben-Gurion declaring the state of Israel, May 14, 1948**

# 74. Chiang Kai-shek
## (1887–1975)

Soldier and statesman, **Chiang Kai-shek** led the Nationalist government in China from 1928 to 1949, when he lost a civil war to the Chinese Communists.

Born in Fenghua, Chekiang province, Chiang was the son of a salt merchant. As a young man, he was educated in military schools in China and Japan. In 1911, joined the forces of revolution and reform inside China. In the aftermath of the revolution, Chiang supported the republican government of Dr. **Sun Yat-sen** (see no. 63), leader of the Nationalist party.

In 1921, when Sun was elected president of the Southern Chinese Republic, Chiang served as his military aide. In 1923, Sun sent Chiang to the Soviet Union to study military organization and to seek aid for the his regime. When Chiang returned, he was appointed commandant of the newly established **Whampoa Military Academy** near Canton. Soviet advisors poured into Canton, and at this time the Chinese Communists were admitted into the Nationalist party.

Chiang's prominence in the Party grew after Sun Yat-sen's death in 1925. However, the Chinese Communists quickly gained strength, and tensions developed between them and the more conservative elements among the Nationalists, led by Chiang. With the Whampoa army behind him, Chiang met this threat with consummate shrewdness, as he attempted to stem the Communists' growing influence without losing Soviet support.

**Chiang Kai-shek**

In 1927, he began a long civil war against the Communists, led by **Mao Tse-tung** (see no. 79), and he lost support from the Soviets. The next year, Chiang became head of the Nationalist government at Nanjing and leader of all Chinese Nationalist forces.

The Communists, the Chinese warlords, and the Japanese all remained a threat to Chiang's government. When war broke out with Japan in 1937, Chiang was compelled to form an alliance with the Communists to fight the Japanese invaders. During World War II, Chiang met with U.S. President **Franklin Roosevelt** and Britain's leader **Winston Churchill**; when the war ended, the Allies recognized Chiang as China's legitimate ruler. However, internally Chiang's government showed signs of decay, and by 1949, he had lost mainland China to Mao's Communists, who established the People's Republic of China.

By 1950, Chiang and the Nationalist government had been driven from the mainland to the island of **Taiwan** (Formosa) where he became a virtual dictator. He reorganized his military forces and then instituted limited democratic reforms. Over the years, Taiwan's economy grew strong, thanks to much support from the United States.

Chiang's international position was weakened considerably in 1971 when the United Nations expelled his regime and accepted the Communists as the sole legitimate government of China. He remained president of Taiwan until his death in 1975.

Regarded as history's most evil dictator, **Adolf Hitler** used his power to build a German war machine that devastated Europe for six years, while he instituted genocidal policies that resulted in the extermination of more than six million Jews.

Adolf Hitler was born in Braunau, Austria. He joined the German Army in World War I, in which he was wounded and awarded the Iron Cross for bravery. In 1919, he helped form the **National Socialist German Workers' party** (or Nazi party), becoming party chairman by 1921.

**Adolf Hitler**

In 1923, Hitler and his supporters attempted to overthrow the Bavarian government during the **Munich** (Beer Hall) **Putsch**. He was arrested and imprisoned, and while in jail, he wrote his political testament, *Mein Kampf* (*My Struggle*), a work full of hatred toward the Jews and ideas of German world domination.

In 1929, Hitler took advantage of the country's economic depression and offered distraught Germans a scapegoat and a solution to their crisis. He promised security to workers, control of trade unions, and revenge against the "Jew financiers" he blamed for Germany's defeat in World War I.

By 1932, the Nazis had gained widespread support. Although Hitler ran unsuccessfully against **Paul von Hindenburg** for president in 1932, the aging leader later appointed Hitler chancellor in an effort to control him. When Hindenburg died in 1934, Hitler combined the presidency and chancellorship and became **Der Führer** (Leader). He suspended the constitution, used secret police, the Gestapo, to silence all opposition, and turned Germany into a fascist state.

In 1938, Hitler annexed both Austria and the Czech Sudetentland to Germany. On September 1, 1939, he ordered the invasion of Poland causing the outbreak of **World War II**. The German army rolled across Europe in the early years of the war; only the resistance of Great Britain and Russia prevented Hitler from conquering the entire continent. By late 1943, with large-scale American assistance, the war had turned in favor of the Allies, as Hitler led Germany down a path of unprecedented destruction.

Throughout the war, Hitler was also determined to rid the continent of Jews. He ordered all Jews deported to concentration camps in Germany and Poland, where many of them were either worked to death or died from horrible conditions. Beginning in the early 1940s, Hitler instituted the "final solution," the extermination of Jews in the camps in gas chambers. By the time the Allies liberated the camps, six million Jews—along with various other "undesirables" such as gypsies and homosexuals—had suffered annihilation.

In April 1945, with the Allied armies closing in, Hitler retreated to a bunker in Berlin where he killed his mistress, Eva Braun, and committed suicide; his aides then burned their bodies.

# 76. Charles de Gaulle
## (1890–1970)

**Charles de Gaulle** led France's resistance to the Nazis during **World War II** and went on to become his nation's president.

Born in Lille, the son of a teacher, de Gaulle was educated at the Military Academy of Saint-Cyr, where he graduated in 1912. He served in World War I, where he was wounded three times and taken prisoner of war. After the war, de Gaulle became a college lecturer, and wrote several books and articles on military subjects.

When World War II broke out, de Gaulle commanded a tank brigade attached to the French 5th army. In May of 1940, he was made a temporary brigadier general, retaining this rank for the rest of his life. When France fell to the Germans in June, de Gaulle strongly opposed the armistice that established the **Vichy** government. He escaped to England, where he became the leader of the French resistance.

In 1943, de Gaulle became head of the French **Committee of National Liberation** in Algiers, the leader of the French government-in-exile. The Allies gave him the privilege of leading French troops into Paris in August 1944 when it was liberated.

In 1945, he was elected president of the provisional government; however, he resigned after ten weeks, following disagreement over the constitution adopted by the Fourth French Republic. By the early 1950s, he had withdrawn from politics and resumed a writing career.

He reentered politics in 1958, when a new constitution was put in place that embodied de Gaulle's conceptions of how France should be governed. Executive power increased considerably at the expense of the National Assembly. De Gaulle was elected president in December 1958, and under the new **Fifth Republic** he appointed a new government.

The most immediate problems facing the new president were the Algerian conflict and an economic crisis at home. De Gaulle pushed through economic recovery measures, and in March 1962, an agreement was reached granting Algeria full independence.

De Gaulle was reelected president in 1965, and began to push France toward an independent foreign policy. To this end, in 1966, he withdrew France from membership in **NATO**, and embarked on a policy of nuclear deterrent. He also signed a historic reconciliation treaty with West Germany, and blocked Britain's entry into the European Economic Community.

Though De Gaulle won an overwhelming victory in the 1968 election, his presidency was severely shaken by the "student revolution" and worker protests that swept France that year. He resigned the following year after his proposed constitutional changes were rejected by the voters.

De Gaulle then retired and resumed the writing of his memoirs. He died in 1970.

**Charles de Gaulle**

General **Francisco Franco** led the Nationalist forces that overthrew the Spanish democratic republic during **Spain's Civil War**, and became dictator of a right-wing government that he controlled until his death.

Franco was born in El Ferrol, Spain, the son of an officer in the Spanish Naval Administrative Corps. As a young man, he graduated from the military academy at Toledo in 1910 and entered the army.

From 1912–1927, Franco commanded troops in Spanish Morocco, helping to suppress a rebellion against colonial domination. At the age of 32, he was promoted to the rank of general, becoming the youngest in his nation at that level.

After the Spanish king abdicated in 1931, the leaders of the new Spanish Republic adopted a sharply antimilitary policy, and Franco's career was temporarily halted. Conservative forces gained control of the republic in 1933, restoring Franco to active command. In 1935, he was appointed chief of the Spanish army's general staff.

After leftists won national elections in 1935, Franco helped lead a military revolt to overthrow the Republican government. Civil War broke out in 1936, and Franco became commander-in-chief of the Nationalist forces. In 1937, he forged the anti-Republican movement under the **Falange** (Fascist) party, which he headed. With major assistance from Europe's two other fascist leaders—Italy's **Mussolini** and Germany's **Hitler**—Franco's army eventually defeated the Republican forces.

In 1939, Franco proclaimed himself leader and took full control of the government. He dealt ruthlessly with his opposition, and established a firmly controlled corporate state. Despite pressure from the Axis powers, and his obvious sympathy toward their cause, Franco kept Spain a nonbelligerent nation in World War II. This was one reason his government survived after the Allies defeated Italy and Germany.

In 1947, he reorganized the government, passing a law of succession that declared Spain a monarchy, naming himself head of state for life. Franco established diplomatic relations with the United States and other members of the United Nations in 1950. During the height of the Cold War, he secured massive U.S. economic aid in return for allowing U.S. military bases in Spain.

From 1959 onward, Franco increasingly depended on the **Roman Catholic Church** to maintain a patriarchal society and control over the population in the countryside. The country's hard times forced him to reluctantly pursue a more liberal economic policy. While the regime was forced to grant some social and political liberties, it remained extreme with regard to the **Basque** provinces, where the government waged a fierce struggle against separatists.

Shortly before Franco's death in November 1975, he named Prince Juan Carlos to rule as king and successor.

**General Franco (right) with Adolf Hitler**

# 78. Haile Selassie I
## (1892–1975)

The last emperor of Ethiopia, **Haile Selassie** sought to modernize his country and make it a leader in post-World War II **Africa**.

He was born Ras (Prince) Tafari Makonnen, near Harer, and was a grandnephew of Emperor Menelik II. In 1911, Makonnen married Wayzaro Menen, Menelik's great granddaughter. The emperor recognized Makonnen's intellectual abilities and promoted him to government office, where he followed progressive policies and developed a salaried civil service. When Menelik's daughter became empress in 1917, Makonnen became regent and heir to the throne.

During the 1920s, he began to essentially control the government. By establishing provincial schools, strengthening the police forces, and outlawing feudal taxation, he sought to both help his people and increase the authority of the central government. In an effort to establish his nation as a modern state, he succeeded in gaining Ethiopia's admission into the **League of Nations** in 1923. He was crowned king in 1928, and upon the death of the empress in 1930, he became emperor, taking the name Haile Selassie I (Might of the Trinity).

In 1931, Selassie granted his subjects a constitution. Although limited, it established a parliament and a court system. When Italy invaded Ethiopia in 1935, Selassie offered resistance, and made an impressive but vain plea for help from the League of Nations. He lost power and went into exile in England. With British assistance, he regained power and returned to Ethiopia in 1942.

After he was reinstated as emperor, Selassie received massive aid from Britain, the United States, and later the United Nations. He implemented programs of economic and educational reform in an attempt to modernize the country. Among his accomplishments were major land reform, emancipation of slaves, and a revised and somewhat broadened constitution that provided for universal suffrage.

Beginning in the 1950s, Selassie also became the focus of a **Rastafarian religious cult**, which regarded him as a divine being who would lead the world's black population back to an earthly paradise in Africa.

**Haile Selassie**

In 1963, Selassie helped found the **Organization of African Unity** (OAU), with its headquarters in Addis Ababa. The OAU promoted the unity and solidarity of African states and the elimination of all forms of colonialism. While the OAU increased his prestige, by 1974, famine, worsening unemployment, and the political stagnation of his government led the army to depose Selassie.

The army established a provisional military government that espoused Marxist ideologies. The monarchy was abolished, and Selassie was kept under house arrest in the palace for the rest of his life. He died in 1975 under unexplained circumstances. Evidence later emerged suggesting that he had been killed on the orders of the military government.

# 79. Mao Tse-tung
## (1893-1976)

**Mao Tse-tung** led the **Communist** takeover of the world's most populous nation and founded the **People's Republic of China**.

Mao was born into a peasant family in Hunan province in 1893. In 1911, he fought in the Chinese Revolution that overthrew the **Manchu** dynasty and resulted in China becoming a republic. By 1919 Mao had converted to **Marxism** and helped found the Chinese Communist party. He also became a political organizer for the Kuomintang, the National People's party formed by Dr. Sun Yat-sen (see no. 63).

When Sun Yat-sen died in 1925, **Chiang Kai-shek** (see no. 74) became the leader of the Kuomintang. Strongly anti-Communist, Chiang expelled most socialists from the Kuomintang, and in 1926, carried out a military coup against the Communists. Mao and his supporters fled to the countryside.

By 1934, Chiang's Nationalist forces had the much smaller Communist army on the run. Mao then led his followers on a 6,000-mile "**Long March**." Perhaps only 4,000 out of some 86,000 men survived the grueling journey to the northern mountains, but the march brought Mao and his supporters international fame and they gained many new recruits.

After the Japanese invasion of China in 1937, the Communists and Nationalists forces forged an uneasy alliance to fight a common enemy. After the Japanese were evicted in 1945, they resumed their conflict. While Chiang's forces held many of the cities,

**Mao Tse-tung**

Mao had overwhelming strength among the peasants in the countryside, and by 1949 the Communists had driven the Nationalists from the mainland. Chiang Kai-shek and his followers retreated to Taiwan, and on October 1, 1949, Mao proclaimed the new Communist state, the People's Republic of China.

In 1950, Mao signed a treaty with the **Soviet Union**, and benefited from Soviet economic aid. Domestically, his **Great Leap Forward** in 1958, a plan for economic and political development, turned the peasants' lives upside down, as enormous new social units replaced their collective farms. The results were disastrous; as many as 20 million people starved.

During the 1960s, Mao initiated another drastic domestic program—the **Cultural Revolution**, which was designed to encourage the spontaneous radicalism of the young and the masses against the entrenched party bureaucracy. To revive Mao's popularity, his staunchest supporters, the **Red Guards**, held parades and put up posters criticizing writers, intellectuals, and other enemies of their leader. This led to a wide cult-like following of Mao.

In the early 1970s, Mao reversed a long-standing anti-U.S. policy and opened a diplomatic dialogue with the United States. He met with President **Richard Nixon** in 1972, and that began an era of better relations with the capitalist West.

By the mid 1970s, Mao's health began to fail, and he died in September 1976.

# 80. Nikita Khrushchev
## (1894–1971)

**Nikita Khrushchev** won a struggle for control of the Soviet Union after the death of Josef Stalin, and was the Soviet leader during the gravest crisis of the **Cold War**.

The son of a coal miner, Khrushchev was born in 1894, in Kalinovka, Ukraine, part of the Russian Empire. He joined the Bolshevik party in 1918, fought in the Russian Civil War, and rose rapidly within the Party organization.

In 1933, he became second secretary of the Moscow Communist party, and was later elected to full membership of the Party's Central Committee. During the 1930s, Khrushchev was a zealous supporter of Stalin and participated in the purges of the Party's leadership. In 1939, Khrushchev was made a full member of the **Politburo**—the highest council of the Soviet government.

During World War II, Khrushchev served in the Red Army, and in the postwar era his political star continued to rise. When Stalin died in March 1953, he was one of five top Soviet officials vying for power. Khrushchev soon emerged in the powerful position of first secretary of the Communist party.

In 1956, at the 20th Party Congress, Khrushchev made a famous speech in which he denounced the crimes of **Stalinism**, the Great Purges, and the "personality cult." The speech provoked an eventual movement to oust Khrushchev from power, but it failed. By the next year, he had removed all his rivals, and added the post of premier to his position as head of the Party.

For the next several years, Khrushchev pursued contradictory policies, especially in foreign affairs. He widely asserted a doctrine of "peaceful coexistence," with the non-Communist world, yet he angered many Western nations with his brutal repression of democracy movements in eastern bloc nations such as Hungary. He toured the United States in 1959, and conferred with President Eisenhower, a move that brought a thaw to U.S.-Soviet relations for the first time in a more than a decade.

**President Eisenhower with Nikita Khrushchev**

However, in 1961, Khrushchev ordered the construction of a wall separating East and West Berlin, closing off access to freedom in the West by East Germans. The next year, he secretly attempted to base Soviet medium-range offensive missiles in **Cuba**, aimed at targets in the United States. After the missiles were detected and President Kennedy demanded they be removed, the two nations stood on the brink of war. Khrushchev finally agreed to remove the missiles on the promise that the United States would make no further attempt to overthrow Cuba's Communist government.

His failures in reforming agriculture policy and the growing rift with Communist China led to Khrushchev's downfall. On October 14, 1964, he was removed from power. He died in Moscow in 1971.

Supported by the working classes and buoyed the popularity of his wife Eva, Argentine dictator **Juan Perón** founded a strongly nationalistic, anti-imperialist movement, and engineered great social reforms during his terms as president.

Perón was born into a modest, lower-middle class family from the Buenos Aires province. He entered military school at age 16, and in 1914 he became a lieutenant in an infantry regiment. During the 1930s, he served as a military attaché to Chile, and in the late 1930s and early 1940s, he visited Italy and Germany to observe fascism first-hand.

**Juan Perón**

Perón's rise to power began in 1943 when he was part of a military coup that overthrew the government of **Ramón Castillo**. The next year he was appointed vice-president and minister of war. In 1945, he married a young radio and film actress named **Maria Eva Duarte**, who would later achieve great popularity and become known as Evita.

Perón was elected president in 1946, with the support of workers, churchmen, and recent migrants from the countryside. He quickly used the post-war economic boom to improve the living conditions of the workers and laborers at the expense of the large landowners. He also nationalized the foreign-controlled railroads and other utilities, and financed public works on a large scale.

At the same time, his wife devoted much of her time and energy to social welfare and the relief of poverty. Extremely popular with the masses, she began to exert strong influence within her husband's government. She organized female workers, secured for women the right to vote, and allocated large amounts of government funds to social welfare programs.

Perón won reelection in 1951, but the next year his wife died from cancer, dealing a severe blow to his government. Over the next few years, as the economy deteriorated, Perón broke with the Catholic Church, and he lost much support among the military. In 1955 he was overthrown by a military coup and forced into exile.

Perón fled to Paraguay and finally settled in Spain. His **Peróniste** movement remained popular at home, however, and it provided support for him during his time in exile. In his absence, Argentina experienced several years of political, social, and economic upheaval.

Perón was allowed to return home in 1971, and was quickly seen by his supporters as a chance to save his country from continuing turmoil. He was elected president again in 1973 with 62 percent of the vote; his third wife, **Isabel Martínez de Perón** was elected vice president.

Perón presided over an economic recovery, but it was short-lived. He died in 1974, and was succeeded by his wife. She was deposed by the army in 1976.

# Golda Meir
## (1898–1978)

**Golda Meir** was one of the founders of the state of **Israel** and later served her nation as prime minister.

She was born Golda Mabovitch in 1898 in Kiev, Russia. When she was eight years old, her family immigrated to Milwaukee, Wisconsin. She was educated at a teacher's seminary and later became a schoolteacher in Milwaukee.

In 1921, she and her husband, Morris Myerson, immigrated to **Palestine** to work and live on a kibbutz; they later changed their surname to the Hebrew, Meir. During the 1920s, Meir became active in both the area of labor relations and in **Zionism**—the movement to create a Jewish state in Palestine. During the 1920s and 1930s, she gained experience as an official of both the Federation of Labor and the Women's Labor Council.

Following World War II, Meir emerged as a forceful spokesperson for the Zionist cause in negotiating with the British authorities. She also worked for the release of the many Jewish war refugees who had violated the British immigration laws by settling in Palestine.

Golda Meir was one of the 25 signatories to Israel's **Proclamation of Independence** issued on May 14, 1948. That same year, she was appointed her country's first ambassador to the Soviet Union. In 1949, she was elected to the first Israeli *Knesset* (Parliament). Dur-ing the early 1950s, she served as minister of Labor and Social Insurance in the government of David Ben-Gurion (see no. 73), and in 1956, she became minister of Foreign Affairs, a post she held for 10 years.

After retiring from the Foreign Ministry in 1966, she became secretary general of the Mapai party and supported Prime Minister Levi Eshkol in party conflicts. After Israel's victory in the Six-Day War in June 1967 against Egypt, Jordan, and Syria, she helped merge Mapai with two dissident parties into the Israel **Labor party**.

Upon Eshkol's death in February 1969, Meir became interim prime minister; after the October 1969 elections, she was elected to a full term. During the next four years, she built a solid international reputation as a tough-minded but empathetic leader.

The major event of her administration was the **Yom Kippur War**, which broke out with massive coordinated Egyptian and Syrian assaults against Israel on October 6, 1973. Israel's lack of readiness for the war, and the number of Israeli casualties stunned the nation, and Meir formed a new coalition government only with great difficulty. Although she and the Labor party won the elections later that year, she resigned in 1974 in favor of Yitzhak Rabin.

Meir published her autobiography, *My Life*, in 1975, and died in 1978, after a 12-year battle with leukemia.

**Golda Meir with President Nixon**

**Ruhollah Hendi** led an Islamic revolution that overthrew the shah of Iran, and became his nation's ultimate political and religious leader.

Hendi was born into a family of Shi'ite scholars in the small town of Khomein, in present-day Iran. Later he dropped his family name and adopted the name of his native village. Like his father, he moved from theological studies to a career as a teacher of religion. He wrote many works on Islamic law and ethics, and as he devoted more of his life to religious studies, he began to be called **ayatollah**, a term of religious distinction.

Throughout the 1940s and 50s, Khomeini watched as Iran's leader (or shah)— **Muhammad Reza Pahlavi**—brought the country closer and closer to the United States and other Western nations, turning it into an increasingly secular state.

Beginning in the early 1960s, Khomeini began to criticize the shah's policies, which he claimed were an adulteration of Islam. For his criticisms, Khomeini was exiled from Iran in 1964. He eventually settled in Iraq, from where he continued to call for the overthrow of the shah.

From the mid-1970s Khomeini's influence inside Iran grew dramatically because of mounting public dissatisfaction with the shah's regime. When Khomeini was forced to leave Iraq in 1978, he settled in a Paris suburb. From there his supporters relayed his tape-recorded messages to an increasingly aroused Iranian populace, and massive civil unrest in late 1978 forced the shah to leave the country in January 1979.

Khomeini arrived in Tehran in triumph in February 1979. Later that year, a referendum on a new constitution created an **Islamic republic** in Iran, with Khomeini named political and religious leader for life. According to Khomeini's dictates, Iranian women were required to wear the veil, Western music and alcohol were banned, and the punishments prescribed by Islamic law were reinstated.

Khomeini's foreign policy included the complete abandonment of the Shah's pro-Western orientation, and particular hostility toward the United States, which had given the shah refuge. In November 1979, Iranian students took 53 American hostages from the U.S. embassy in Teheran, sparking a crisis that would last for 444 days. Khomeini provoked outrage in the West by not demanding that the students free the hostages.

Over the remaining decade of his life, Khomeini consolidated his rule. Proving himself as ruthless as the shah had been, he had thousands killed while stamping out a rebellion of the secular left. Iran's course of economic development foundered under Khomeini's rule, and his pursuit of victory in the Iran-Iraq War ultimately proved futile. Khomeini was able to retain his charismatic hold over Iran's Shi'ite masses until his death, which sparked an outpouring of grief.

**Ayatollah Khomeini**

# 84. Achmad Sukarno
## (1901–1970)

**Achmad Sukarno** was the founder and leader of the Indonesian Nationalist movement and became the first president of an independent Indonesia.

Sukarno was born in Java, in the Dutch East Indies, the son of a poor schoolteacher. At the age of 15, Sukarno was sent away to secondary school and to lodgings in the home of Omar Said Tjokroaminoto, a prominent civic and religious figure. Tjokroaminoto financed his further education, and married him off at age 20 to his own 16-year-old daughter, Siti Utari.

Endowed with a commanding presence and supreme self-confidence, Sukarno helped form the radical **Indonesia Nationalist party** in 1927. He was imprisoned for his activities by the Dutch colonial authorities from 1929 to 1931, and then exiled to Sumatra. He returned to Jakarta in 1942, after the Japanese occupation, which he supported in return for their recognition of his leadership of the nationalist movement. By the end of the war, when the collapse of Japan became imminent, Sukarno declared Indonesia's independence in August 1945.

As president of the shaky new republic, Sukarno united the resistance forces against the Netherlands, who were anxious to reclaim their former colony. After four years, the nationalist movement succeeded, and the Dutch formally transferred sovereignty in December 1949. As Indonesia's first president, Sukarno's task was to bring together a disparate population scattered across islands extending over more than 3,000 miles in the Pacific and Indian oceans.

During the first several years of his reign, there were impressive gains in health, education, and cultural self-awareness. However, at the same time, the Indonesian economy foundered while Sukarno conducted numer-

**Achmad Sukarno**

ous receptions, banquets, concerts, and other expensive cultural events.

In the late 1950s, regional and factional problems led Sukarno to replace the 1945 constitution, dissolve parliamentary democracy, and replace it with so-called "guided democracy;" he now became a dictator. Sukarno soon increased his country's ties to **Communist China**, and his protestations of political "neutralism" were offset by his increasingly virulent anti-Western foreign policy. In 1963, he declared himself president for life. In January 1965, Indonesia formally withdrew from the United Nations because the world organization supported Malaysia, which Sukarno had vowed to "crush."

During the mid-1960s, Sukarno's personal and political excesses, and a corruption scandal in his cabinet, induced a continuous state of national crisis. In 1965, he narrowly escaped a coup d'etat by a clique of communist conspirators. The coup resulted in student rioting in the streets, and antimilitary forces led by General **Hadji Suharto**, restored order after massacring hundreds of Communist sympathizers.

In 1966, Sukarno was forced to delegate wide powers to Suharto, who subsequently became acting president. Sukarno lived under house arrest until his death in 1970.

# 85. Hirohito
## (1901–1989)

**Hirohito**

During Emperor **Hirohito's** turbulent 63–year reign Japan went from a military and imperialist power bent on dominating Asia to a defeated, devastated nation, in the process causing the role of the emperor in Japanese life to change forever.

Michinomiya Hirohito was born in Tokyo, the 124th direct descendant of Jimmu, Japan's first emperor. Hirohito was the eldest son of Crown Prince Yoshihito, the future Emperor Taishō.

In 1921, Hirohito visited Europe, becoming the first Japanese crown prince to travel abroad. For the first time the young man experienced personal freedom, visiting museums, fishing in a Scottish lake, and shopping in Paris. When he returned to Japan, he was named prince regent when his father retired because of mental illness. In 1924 Hirohito married the princess **Nagako Kuni**. In 1926, Hirohito's father died, and he was crowned emperor.

Though the Japanese constitution invested Hirohito with supreme authority, in practice he merely ratified the policies of his ministers and advisors. His reign was marked by rapid

militarization, and aggressive wars against **Manchuria** in 1931 and **China** in 1937. Then in 1941, Japan shocked the world with a surprise attack on U.S. military forces in **Pearl Harbor**, Hawaii, provoking a war with America—and dragging Japan into World War II.

Some historians assert that Hirohito did not want war with the United States and that he opposed Japan's alliance with Germany and Italy, but was powerless to resist the militarists who dominated the armed forces and the government. Others believe that Hirohito might have been planning Japan's expansionist policies from 1931 until World War II. Wherever the truth lies, Hirohito made an unprecedented radio broadcast announcing Japan's unconditional surrender to the Allies on August 15, 1945, after atomic bombs were dropped on both Hiroshima and Nagasaki. For many Japanese, this was the first time they heard their emperor speak.

In a second historic broadcast, made on January 1, 1946, Hirohito repudiated the traditional quasi-divine status of Japan's emperors. The constitution of 1946 made him "symbol of the state and of the unity of the people." Hirohito's new role was instrumental in America's occupation and successful program for the democratization of Japan.

After the war, many long-standing royal traditions were set aside. The emperor became familiar as a marine biologist, family figure, and greeter of foreign heads of state. He allowed photographs of his family to be taken. In 1959 his oldest son, Crown Prince Akihito, married a commoner, Shoda Michiko, breaking a 1,500-year tradition.

In 1971 Hirohito toured Europe, becoming the first reigning Japanese monarch to travel abroad. In 1975 he made a state visit to the United States. Upon his death in 1989, Akihito succeeded him as emperor.

# 86. Dag Hammarskjöld
## (1905–1961)

Sweden's **Dag Hammarskjöld** served as the second secretary-general of the **United Nations**, and greatly enhanced the prestige and effectiveness of the world organization.

Dag Hammarskjöld was the fourth son of Hjalmar Hammarskjöld, Prime Minister of Sweden during World War I. The young Hammarskjöld was brought up in the university town of Uppsala. By the age of 25, he had received a Bachelor of Arts degree, a degree in economics, and had become a Bachelor of Laws; he later taught political economics at Stockholm University. He then joined the Swedish civil service.

In 1947, he was appointed to the Foreign Office, where he was responsible for all economic questions with a rank of undersecretary. He was a delegate to the Paris conference in 1947 when the Marshall Plan machinery was established. In 1951, Hammarskkjöld was chosen vice chairman of Sweden's delegation to the UN General Assembly, of which he became chairman in 1952.

On April 10, 1953, five months after the resignation of Norway's Trygve Lie as secretary-general, Hammarskjöld was elected to the office for a term of five years. In September 1957, he was reelected to a second five-year term.

During his tenure as secretary-general, Hammarskjöld carried out many responsibilities for the United Nations in its efforts to prevent war and serve the other aims of the UN Charter. For several years he was most concerned with the conflict in the **Middle East** between Israel and the Arab states and promoted progress toward more peaceful conditions in the area. In 1956, he helped formulate the resolution of the **Suez Canal** crisis between Egypt and the Western nations.

In 1955, following his visit to Beijing, China released 15 detained American fliers who had served under the United Nations Command in the Korean War.

As secretary-general, Hammarskjold traveled to many countries around the world. He earned a reputation for combining great moral force with personal subtlety in meeting international challenges. When the **Belgian Congo** became the independent Republic of the Congo on June 30, 1960, he sent a UN military force to suppress the civil strife that erupted there. In September 1960, the Soviet Union denounced his action and demanded his removal from office. Hammarskjöld insisted however, he had the authority to take emergency action without prior approval by the Security Council or the General Assembly. Later, the General Assembly in an overwhelming vote, approved of Hammarskjöld's actions in the Congo.

Hammarskjöld made four trips to the Congo in connection with the United Nations operations there. In returning from his fourth trip on September 18, 1961, he was killed in a plane crash. He was posthumously awarded the **Nobel Peace Prize.**

**Dag Hammarskjöld**

The first Black African to lead his country to independence from British colonial rule, **Kwame Nkrumah** inspired a generation of Black African leaders.

Nkrumah was born in the British colony of the Gold Coast (present-day Ghana). Baptized and educated as a Roman Catholic, he later taught at Catholic junior schools and at a seminary. An increasing interest in politics led him to pursue further studies in the United States.

After teaching political science for a time, Nkrumah left the United States in May 1945, and went to England. In London, he met several Black African leaders campaigning for independence from British colonial rule.

**Kwame Nkrumah**

Nkrumah returned home in 1947, and he became president of the newly-formed **United Gold Coast Convention party** (UGCC). Nkrumah soon began an intense campaign for self-rule. Boycotts of European goods were initiated; labor strikes became commonplace, and work slowdowns began. When extensive riots occurred in February 1948, the British briefly arrested Nkrumah and other UGCC leaders.

By 1949, Nkrumah had become impatient with what he felt was the slowness of the independence movement. So in June he formed the more radical **Convention Peoples party** (CPP). In January 1950, he began a campaign of "positive action," involving nonviolent protests, strikes, and noncooperation with the British colonial authorities. Nkrumah was again arrested and this time he was sentenced to one year's imprisonment.

In 1951, the CPP won an overwhelming victory in the legislative elections, and the British were forced to release Nkrumah from prison. In 1952, the assembly elected him the first prime minister of the Gold Coast.

In March 1957, the Gold Coast became the first Black African colony to achieve independence, adopting the name Ghana, and Nkrumah became its leader. His style of government proved to be authoritarian. However, his popularity rose as new roads, schools, and health facilities were built, and as the policy of **Africanization** created better lives for the people. In addition, Nkrumah traveled widely, encouraging other African states to become independent.

By the early 1960s, Nkrumah's government had become involved in magnificent but often-ruinous development projects, so that a once-prosperous country became crippled with foreign debt. Contraction of the economy led to widespread labor unrest and to a general strike in September 1961.

In August 1962, Nkrumah survived the first of several assassination attempts. Early in 1964, he declared Ghana officially a one-party state, banned all opposition parties, and named himself president for life. However, by 1966, he had become so unpopular, that in February, while he was visiting Beijing, the army and police in Ghana deposed him and seized power. He found asylum in Guinea, and later moved to Romania, where he died of cancer in 1972.

# Ronald Reagan
(1911– )

Ronald Reagan parlayed a career in Hollywood into politics, rising to become president of the United States as the leader of a conservative "revolution" during the 1980s.

Reagan was born in Tampico, Illinois, in 1911. After college, he embarked on a career as a radio sports announcer. In 1937, he was signed to a movie contract and went to Holly-wood. Over the next 30 years, he starred in several "B" movies and hosted two dramatic television series. During this period, he was married twice—first to actress Jane Wyman, and then after their divorce, to actress Nancy Davis.

A one-time liberal Democrat, Reagan became a **Republican** in 1962, and a leading conservative. In 1966 he was elected governor of California; he was reelected to a second term in 1970.

After failing twice to gain the Republican presidential nomination, Reagan succeeded in winning it in 1980. At 69 years-old, Reagan was one of the oldest candidates to run for the office. However, his exuberance and optimism during the campaign overcame voters' doubts, and his criticisms of an increasingly unpopular president, Jimmy Carter, hit home with many voters. Reagan won the election handily, 489 electoral votes to 49 for Carter.

Two months after assuming office, Reagan was nearly killed when an assassin shot him at close range as he was leaving a Washington hotel. His good humor and courage, and his remarkable speedy recovery, engendered much good will with the American people.

Reagan came to office promising to cut taxes, trim "wasteful government programs," and restore American prestige abroad. By the mid-1980s, he had fulfilled much of his promises. At the same time, Reagan also dramatically increased defense spending, a move that was heavily criticized by those who claimed that it would cause enormous budget deficits; that claim proved to be correct.

However, despite a brief recession in 1982, Reagan remained immensely popular. In 1984, he won reelection by the largest landslide in history, defeating Democrat **Walter Mondale** by 17 million votes.

During his second term, Reagan surprised many people by developing a strong working partnership with **Mikhail Gorbachev**, the new leader of the Soviet Union. The two reached agreements on destroying medium-ranged missiles, dramatically eased East-West tensions, and paved the way for the eventual end of the Cold War.

Reagan's second term was marked by some controversy, especially the **Iran-Contra affair**, where Reagan's subordinates took money from illegal arms sales to Iran and used them to fund a counterrevolutionary Nicaraguan group despite Congressional prohibition.

However, when he left office in 1989, Reagan remained hugely popular with the American people. In 1994, many Americans were saddened to learn that he was suffering from Alzheimer's disease.

**Mikhail Gorbachev and President Reagan**

# 89. Richard Nixon
## (1913–1994)

No one in 20th century American politics had a more spectacular rise and a more dramatic fall than **Richard Nixon**, who in 1974 became the first U.S. president to resign from office.

Richard Nixon was born in Yorba Linda, California. He entered politics in his home state in 1946, running as a **Republican** and winning a seat in Congress. In 1950, he won a Senate race against the incumbent Democrat, Helen Gahagan Douglas.

**Richard Nixon**

In 1952, Nixon continued his meteoric rise by being picked as Republican presidential nominee Dwight D. Eisenhower's running mate. Eisenhower was elected twice, and during Nixon's eight years as vice president, he did not assume any significant responsibilities.

Nixon received his party's presidential nomination in 1960 and ran against Democrat **John F. Kennedy**, to whom he lost the election by a very small margin. Eight years later, Nixon made a startling political comeback and captured the Republican presidential nomination. He then defeated Democrat **Hubert Humphrey** in a race that was nearly as close as the one he lost to Kennedy.

Nixon came to office with the country torn apart by the **Vietnam War** and beset with domestic unrest and violence. Aiming to achieve "peace with honor" in Vietnam, Nixon gradually reduced U.S. troop strength there, while also escalating the war into neighboring nations such as Cambodia. Eventually, however, in January 1973, a peace agreement was signed in Paris that ended U.S. involvement in the war. In domestic affairs, his administration instituted a number of reforms in welfare policy, law enforcement, and the environment.

In 1972 , Nixon was reelected in a landslide over **George McGovern**. In early 1973, however, his second administration began to unravel. On June 17, 1972, five employees of Nixon's reelection committee had been arrested in a break-in for trying to plant surveillance equipment inside the Democratic party National Headquarters in the **Watergate** building in Washington, D.C. Evidence was later uncovered that linked several top White House aides with either initiating the break-in, or with later attempts to conceal the fact that the men involved had close ties to the White House.

Nixon insisted that he had no knowledge of either the break-in or of a cover-up. However, after investigations by Congress and a special prosecutor, it was revealed that he could be heard on taped conversations in the Oval Office six days after the crime, discussing ways to obstruct the investigation of the break-in.

In July 1974, the **House Judiciary Committee** voted to impeach Nixon for obstruction of justice. Realizing he would be convicted in the Senate and removed from office, Nixon resigned in disgrace, on August 8, 1974.

Nixon returned to California, went into seclusion, and wrote his memoirs. He died in 1994.

# 90. John F. Kennedy
## (1917–1963)

Young, vigorous, and charismatic, **John F. Kennedy** came to office with great promise, only to have his presidency end tragically at the hands of an assassin.

John Fitzgerald Kennedy was born in Brookline, Massachusetts, the son of Joseph Patrick Kennedy, a multimillionaire, and Rose Fitzgerald, daughter of a former Boston mayor.

He graduated from Harvard in 1940, and entered the Navy. During World War II, he was cited for heroism for rescuing the crew of his PT boat after it had been smashed by a Japanese destroyer. After the war, Kennedy was elected to Congress as a Democrat from Boston. In 1952, he advanced to the Senate, where he served for eight years. In 1953, he married Jacqueline Bouvier, the daughter of a socialite.

In 1960, Kennedy captured the Democratic nomination for president. Millions watched his television debates with Republican candidate, **Richard Nixon**. In the closest popular election in history, Kennedy won by the slimmest of margins; at 43, he was the nation's youngest elected president, as well as the first Roman Catholic.

Kennedy came to office promising to bring a new, invigorating spirit to Washington. He initiated programs such as the **Peace Corps** and the **Alliance for Progress** to help bring American democracy to developing nations. He pressed Congress to pass tax cuts, improve labor conditions, and in 1963, submitted the most sweeping civil rights legislation in the nation's history.

**John F. Kennedy**

In foreign affairs, Kennedy faced several crises as **Cold War** tensions with the Soviet Union reached new heights. In 1961, he was forced to admit responsibility in a failed CIA-backed effort to overthrow Cuban leader Fidel Castro. Later that year, the Soviets erected the **Berlin Wall,** cutting off East Berlin from the democratic West. The United States took a strong stand against the Soviet action, but was powerless to prevent it.

The most serious crisis of his presidency came in October 1962, with the discovery that the Soviets were placing medium-range nuclear missiles in **Cuba**, 90 miles from America. Kennedy ordered a naval blockade of the island and demanded that Soviet leader **Nikita Khrushchev** (see no. 80) order the missiles dismantled. After ten days of tense negotiations, the standoff ended when Khrushchev agree to the demand in return for a U.S. guarantee not to invade Cuba.

In early planning for the 1964 presidential campaign, Kennedy traveled to Texas in November 1963. While driving in a motorcade through Dallas on November 22, he was shot in the head and died within an hour.

Although many conspiracy theories have been advanced over the years, the crime was blamed solely on a disgruntled ex-Marine turned Communist named Lee Harvey Oswald, who was himself killed two days after killing Kennedy.

# 91. Indira Gandhi
## (1917–1984)

The first woman prime minister of India, **Indira Gandhi** dedicated her life to political and social progress in her country.

Indira Gandhi was born in Allahabad, India, the only child of Jawaharlal Nehru, the first prime minister of independent India. She was educated in India and Europe, and then she entered politics. She joined the National Congress party in 1938 and became active in India's independence movement. In 1942, she married **Feroze Gandhi**, with whom she had two sons.

After India gained independence in 1947, she began to work at her father's side, and rose through the ranks of the Congress party. In 1964, upon her father's death, she became minister of information and broadcasting in the government of Prime Minister Shastri. When Shastri died in 1966, she became prime minister.

Indira Gandhi

Gandhi gained enormous popularity by her actions during the Pakistani civil war (1971); with her support, the East Pakistanis finally achieved independence and became the nation of Bangladesh. She also earned support by promising to use scientific methods to eradicate poverty.

Gandhi was overwhelmingly reelected in 1971, but problems soon began to plague her government. Shortly after the election, her opponent charged that she had violated the election laws and her leadership became vulnerable. A sharp economic downturn caused by severe droughts led to widespread unrest.

In June 1975, responding to what she said was a threat to national security, she declared a national state of emergency; political opponents were imprisoned, the press was censored, and civil liberties were limited.

During this period, she also implemented several unpopular policies, including large-scale, voluntary sterilization to control the rising population. When national elections were held in 1977, Gandhi and her party were soundly defeated, and she left office. Later that year, she was briefly jailed on charges of political corruption, and later she was expelled from Parliament.

However, the new government failed to solve India's problems. By 1980, Gandhi had reorganized her party, and in the elections that year, she became prime minister again. When her son **Sanjay**, her chief political advisor, died in a plane crash, she began grooming her older son, **Rajiv**, as her successor.

Gandhi's second term was beset by religious disturbances and terrorism caused by separatists. Several states sought a larger measure of independence from the central government, and **Sikh** extremists in the **Punjab** violently asserted their demands for an autonomous state. In 1984, she moved vigorously to suppress Sikh insurgents by sending troops to storm the **Golden Temple** in Amritsar, killing more than 300 people. In retaliation, on October 31, 1984, Sikh members of her security guard shot her to death.

# 92. Ferdinand Marcos
## (1917–1989)

**Ferdinand Marcos** was a political leader and longtime dictator of the Philippines, whose repressive regime was finally overthrown by a "people's power" movement during the 1980s.

Ferdinand Marcos was born into a well-to-do family in Sarrat, Philippines in 1917. During **World War II**, he was an officer with the Philippine armed forces and helped lead the resistance against the Japanese. He was elected to the House of Representatives in 1949 as a member of the Liberal party; in 1959, he won election to the Senate.

Marcos broke with the Liberal party in 1965. That year he ran for president as a nominee of the Nationalist party and was elected. He was reelected in 1969, the first Philippine president to win a second term.

As president, Marcos kept close ties with the **United States** and launched major military campaigns against local **Communist rebels** as well as against Moro rebels (Muslims) in **Mindanao**, an island in the south Philippines. During his first term, though he made progress in agriculture, industry, and education, student demonstrations and violent urban-guerrilla activities increased.

Civil strife also marked his second term, and in 1972, following a series of bombings in Manila, he warned of an imminent Communist takeover. That September, he declared martial law and his regime became more repressive. Secret pro-Marcos groups terrorized and even murdered his opponents. Thousands more were arrested and strict censorship of the press was practiced.

In 1973, he assumed virtual dictatorial control. Widespread corruption and the extravagance of his wife, **Imelda**, fed his regime's increasing isolation. Imelda became a powerful figure, and was often criticized for appointing her relatives to government positions.

**Ferdinand Marcos**

A strong opposition movement arose, led by **Benigno Aquino**. After being jailed and detained for eight years, Aquino was exiled and spent three years in the United States. He returned to the Philippines in 1983 to lead the anti-Marcos movement again. As he stepped off the plane, Aquino was gunned down and killed. Marcos insisted he knew nothing about the murder, but the assassination set off new anti-government riots and protests calling for Marcos' ouster.

The opposition then united behind Aquino's widow, **Corazon Aquino**, who led a "people's power" movement and ran against Marcos in the February 1986 election. Marcos declared himself the winner, but Aquino charged that he had stolen the election.

Soon some of Marcos' closest aides came forward and charged that he had rigged the election and had ordered the murder of Benigno Aquino. With his health failing, and even former allies such as the United Sates urging him to resign, Marcos and his family fled the country and went into exile in Hawaii, where he died in 1989.

# 93. Gamal Abdel Nasser
## (1918–1970)

**Gamal Abdel Nasser**

**Gamal Abdel Nasser** rose from a modest upbringing to become president of Egypt, and his efforts to unify the Arab nations made him a national hero and the acknowledged leader of the Arab world.

Nasser was born in a mud-brick house in Alexandria, Egypt, where his father was in charge of the local post office. From Alexandria, Nasser's father was transferred to al-Khatatibah, a squalid delta village, where the young boy began school. He then went to live in Cairo with an uncle and entered the **Cairo Military Academy**, graduating as a second lieutenant. He fought in the unsuccessful Arab war against Israel in 1948.

With three fellow officers, Nasser formed a secret revolutionary organization, the **Free Officers**, whose aim was to overthrow King Farouk. After Egypt's humiliation in the war against Israel, the movement grew quickly. In July 1952, Nasser and 89 other Free Officers staged an almost bloodless coup d'etat that ended with the king and his supporters going into exile. The Revolutionary Command Council took over the country; General **Mohammad Neguib** became president and Nasser became minister of the interior and Neguib's deputy. Nasser then engaged in a bitter power struggle with Neguib, and replaced him as president in 1954.

In January 1956, Nasser announced a constitution under which Egypt became a socialist Arab state with a one-party political system and with **Islam** as the official religion. Nasser then began to reduce government corruption, and carry out some land and social reforms. His announcement, in 1956, of his intention to nationalize the **Suez Canal** was highly popular at home, but set off an international crisis. Great Britain, with help from France and Israel attacked Egypt, but in the aftermath of the brief war, Nasser emerged with undiminished prestige throughout the Arab world.

With the United States and other Western nations following a strong pro-Israeli policy, Nasser turned toward the **Soviet Union** for assistance. He purchased arms from the Soviets, and used Soviet funds to help construct the **Aswan High Dam**, which would help introduce modern 20th century life to many Egyptian villages.

In 1967, Nasser led the Arab nations against Israel in what became known as the **Six-Day War**. In the wake of Israel's overwhelming success, Nasser briefly resigned as president; however, his continued popularity with the Egyptian people brought him back to power.

Despite his international setbacks, Nasser accomplished much at home during his tenure. He redistributed land, encouraged industrialization, and expanded public works, as well as providing more equitable educational opportunities.

Nasser died of a heart attack in 1970, just one year before the completion of his greatest domestic project, the Aswan High Dam.

# 94. Anwar Sadat
## (1918–1981)

As president of Egypt, **Anwar Sadat** helped end 30 years of Egyptian-Israeli hostilities, and brought a measure of peace to the Middle East for the first time in modern history.

Sadat was born in a small village in the Nile delta, the son of a hospital clerk. He graduated from the **Cairo Military Academy** in 1938, and was sent to a distant outpost where he met **Gamal Abdel Nasser**. During World War II, Sadat was imprisoned for plotting to expel the British from Egypt. He escaped, and after the war, he joined Nasser's group, the **Free Officers**, which was dedicated to overthrowing the British-dominated monarchy.

In 1952, Sadat joined the Free Officers' armed coup that resulted in the overthrow of King Farouk. Sadat supported Nasser's election to the presidency in 1956, and over the next decade, served in a number of important posts, including minister of state. In 1969, Sadat was chosen as Nasser's vice president, and he became president the next year after Nasser's death.

In an effort to remove himself from Nasser's huge shadow, Sadat began to decentralize the country's political structure and diversify the economy. He also distanced himself from Nasser's foreign policy by expelling Soviet technicians and advisors from the country and initiating closer ties with the United States.

In 1973, Sadat launched the **Yom-Kippur War** against Israel, which caught the Israelis unprepared and restored some of the Egyptian honor lost during the humiliation of the 1967 Six-Day War. With his prestige at home quite high, Sadat made a dramatic turnaround and began to work toward peace in the Middle East. He made a historic visit to Israel in November 1977, and addressed the Israeli Parliament. The trip initiated a series of diplomatic efforts that Sadat continued despite enormous opposition from most of the Arab world.

U.S. President Jimmy Carter mediated the negotiations between Sadat and Israeli Prime Minister **Menachem Begin** that resulted in the Camp David Accords of September 1978. The agreement established a framework for continuing negotiations that resulted in a peace treaty between Egypt and Israel in March 1979, the first treaty between Israel and any Arab nation. For their efforts, Sadat and Begin shared the **Nobel Peace Prize** for 1978.

**Anwar Sadat**

At home, Sadat's new relationship with the West and his peace treaty generated domestic opposition, especially among fundamentalist Muslim groups. In 1980 and 1981, Sadat took desperate measures to respond to these internal problems. He negotiated a number of loans to improve everyday life, while at the same time cracking down on the opposition by outlawing protests. Despite these actions, Sadat was assassinated by Muslim extremists while reviewing a military parade in October 1981.

# 95. Nelson Mandela
## (1918– )

**Nelson Mandela** endured lengthy imprisonment during his lifetime struggle against South Africa's **apartheid** system, and triumphed by becoming his nation's first elected black president.

Nelson Rolihlahla Mandela was born in 1918 in Cape of Good Hope, South Africa. He was the son of Chief Henry Mandela of the Thembu people. As a young man, Mandela moved to Johannesburg, earned a law degree, and became active in Youth League, a wing of the **African National Congress** (ANC), a Black Nationalist group. In 1949, Mandela became a leader in the ANC and engaged in militant resistance against the new white ruling National Party's policies of apartheid, which now officially segregated the black population and denied them basic rights all white South Africans enjoyed.

In 1953, Mandela was banned for his ANC activities, and in 1956, he was tried for treason. The trial lasted five years, and Mandela was eventually acquitted. During this period, he divorced his first wife and married **Nomzamo Winifred (Winnie) Madikizela**, a social worker.

After the **Sharpeville Massacre** in 1960, in which government troops killed and wounded scores of peaceful black demonstrators, Mandela organized a paramilitary group to engage in guerrilla warfare against the government. In 1962, he was jailed and sentenced to five years in prison. Then in 1963, Mandela and several other men were tried for treason and sabotage. In June, 1964, he was

**Nelson and Winnie Mandela**

convicted and sentenced to life in prison.

Throughout the 1970s and 1980s, Mandela maintained wide support among South Africa's black population. He also gained further support within the international community, largely due to the efforts of his wife, Winnie, who was instrumental in making him the leading symbol of South African repression. By the late 1980s, there was growing international pressure for his release. In 1989, President **F. W. de Klerk** began the process of dismantling apartheid.

Mandela was released from prison in February 1990, as an expression of de Klerk's commitment to change.

Mandela and the ANC began negotiations with the government to end white majority rule in South Africa. Mandela and de Klerk were jointly awarded the **Nobel Peace Prize** in 1993 for their work in bringing about a peaceful transition to nonracial democracy in South Africa.

In South Africa's first multiracial elections in 1994, Mandela was elected president. He investigated human rights violations under apartheid and introduced housing, education, and economic development initiatives designed to improve the living standards of the country's black population.

In 1996, Mandela and his wife divorced, after she had become a controversial figure, accused of being an accessory to criminal activities committed by her bodyguards. In 1999 Mandela did not seek a second term as president, and retired from active politics.

As Great Britain's first woman prime minister, **Margaret Thatcher's** rigid approach to policy making and steely self-confidence earned her the title— from friend and foe alike—the "Iron Lady."

She was born Margaret Hilda Roberts in Lincolnshire, England. She was educated at Oxford University, where she became interested in politics. In 1951, she married **Denis Thatcher**, a wealthy businessman.

With her husband's encouragement, Mrs. Thatcher pursued her political ambitions. In 1959, she became a member of Parliament as a **Conservative**. From 1970 to 1974, she served as minister of education and science under Prime Minister Edward Heath.

In 1975, Thatcher became leader of the Conservative party, the first woman to hold that position. By the late 1970s, Britain was going through very tough times. In March 1979, Thatcher called for a no-confidence vote in the ruling Labor party leadership. When elections were held in May, the Conservatives won a majority and Margaret Thatcher became Great Britain's first woman prime minister.

To boost the economy, she announced lower income-tax rates and cut social programs. While this action pleased conservatives, she was also heavily criticized by others for being cold-hearted toward the jobless and the poor.

Unemployment, which had been rising mildly throughout the late 1970s, climbed dramatically by 1981, bringing riots throughout the country. Thatcher's reaction was to crack down with more police enforcement. During her time in office, she also privatized some nationalized industries and social programs, including education, housing, and health care. While Thatcher's policies continued to draw criticism, the economy improved throughout much of the 1980s, and she was given credit for it.

In 1982, Argentine forces occupied the nearby **Falkland Islands**, which were claimed by both Argentina and Great Britain. Thatcher's government sent a task force to the islands that defeated the Argentineans in a brief war. Her Falkland Islands success, and the economic upturn, allowed Thatcher to lead the Conservatives to a sweeping victory in the elections of 1983, giving her a second term as prime minister.

Throughout the 1980s, Thatcher developed a close working relationship with U.S. President **Ronald Reagan** (see no. 88), who shared many of her conservative views. Thatcher was also one of the first Western leaders to meet with Soviet president **Mikhail Gorbachev**, and announced that he was a leader the West could "do business with."

In 1987, Thatcher won an unprecedented third term as prime minister. However, by 1990, a recession had set in. Then controversy over Thatcher's tax policy, and her reluctance to commit Great Britain to full economic integration with Europe, inspired a strong internal challenge to her leadership. She resigned as head of the Conservative party late in 1990. She was succeeded as leader and prime minister by her protégé, John Major.

**Margaret Thatcher**

# 97. Fidel Castro
## (1926– )

A lawyer turned revolutionary, **Fidel Castro** transformed Cuba into the first Communist nation in the Western Hemisphere.

Fidel Castro was born in Cuba's Mayari municipality, the son of a sugarcane farmer. As a youth, Castro attended Catholic schools and studied law at Havana University, graduating in 1950.

After law school, Castro went to work in Havana, helping the poor. By the early 1950s, he had come to detest the regime of Cuba's dictator, **Fulgencio Batista**, whose harsh rule favored the wealthy class. Castro became involved in revolutionary politics, and in 1953, he helped lead an unsuccessful attempt to overthrow Batista. Castro was jailed and spent two years in prison before being released in 1955. He then went into exile to organize a guerrilla campaign to oust Batista.

In December 1956, a group led by Castro, his brother Raul, and another committed revolutionary, **Ernesto "Che" Guevara**, organized another attempt to overthrow Batista. Once again they failed, and they retreated to the mountains. For the next two years, with Castro's charismatic leadership, the movement to overthrow the dictatorship gathered support, until finally, on January 1, 1959, they toppled Batista. He fled the country—and Castro and his forces triumphantly entered Havana to take control.

Widely hailed as a liberator, Castro proved to be a tough and often ruthless leader. He collectivized agriculture and took over foreign-owned industries. He instituted sweeping reforms in favor of the poor, disenfranchising the propertied classes, many of whom fled the country. These policies, along with Castro's trade agreement with the **Soviet Union** in February 1960 deepened distrust in the United States, which broke diplomatic relations with Cuba in 1961.

In April 1961, the United States organized an invasion of Cuban exiles at the **Bay of Pigs**, which was a disastrous failure. A year later, the world came to the brink of nuclear war when the Soviet Union, now the island nation's chief supporter and trade partner, placed nuclear weapons there capable of reaching the United States. The crisis was defused following negotiations between the superpowers and the removal of the missiles.

Castro maintained his iron grip on power throughout the next three decades. While the quality of life for the poorest people improved, there was no denying that Cubans had lost many of their basic freedoms as Castro refused to allow any democratic opposition to his rule.

**Fidel Castro**

When the Soviet Union collapsed in 1991, Cuba entered a crisis period. Popular unrest grew in the face of extreme austerity measures. In desperate need of foreign capital, Castro opened Cuba to foreign investment and promoted tourism, while further clamping down on dissent. Though his prestige dwindled dramatically, Castro remained a symbol of revolutionary progress for many of Cuba's poorest citizens.

# 98. Mikhail Gorbachev
## (1931– )

**Mikhail Gorbachev** brought dramatic changes to the Soviet Union during the 1980s, and then allowed a wildfire democracy movement to sweep across Eastern Europe and end the Cold War.

Born to farming parents in a Russian village along the Volga River, Mikhail Gorbachev also worked in the fields as a young boy. His father was a Communist party official, and by 1946 the young man had joined the Komsomol (Communist Youth League). Gorbachev went on to study law at Moscow University and graduated in 1955. During the early 1950s, he also joined the Communist party and married Raisa Maksimovna Titorenko.

Returning to Stavropol, he began to move up within the Party ranks. By 1978, he had moved to Moscow to further his career. In 1980, Gorbachev became a full member of the **Politburo**, the national Soviet governing body, and by 1983, he had been given full responsibility for the economy, which had been stagnating for many years. In 1985, despite his relative young age, Gorbachev succeeded Konstantin Chernenko as general secretary of the Communist party, the nation's top leadership position.

From the beginning, Gorbachev cultivated warmer relations and trade with the developed nations of both West and East. He also helped usher in a new era of good relations with the United States by holding a series of summit talks with President **Ronald Reagan** that led both countries to sign an Intermediate Nuclear Forces (INF) arms limitation treaty in 1987. Most dramatically, in 1989, when democracy movements swept across Eastern Europe in Soviet-dominated countries, Gorbachev refused to follow the actions of previous leaders and suppress them. By not taking action, he effectively helped end the Cold War, culminating in the fall of the Berlin Wall that year.

Internally, Gorbachev embarked on a dual policy of social and political reform, *glasnost* (openness), along with *perestroika* (economic restructuring). Though the changes greatly democratized Soviet politics and increased cultural and social freedoms, they produced few economic benefits; at the same time, the reforms unleashed long-suppressed ethnic conflicts and separatist movements.

The signing of a treaty transferring many powers to the republics within the Soviet Union led hard-liners in Gorbachev's government to temporarily oust him from power. In the aftermath, Gorbachev aligned himself with **Boris Yeltsin**, who had helped thwart the takeover. Gorbachev resigned from the Communist party, and though he agreed to even greater power sharing with the republics, these efforts failed to prevent the Soviet Union's disintegration. On December 25, 1991, Gorbachev resigned, and a week later the Soviet Union ceased to exist.

Mikhail Gorbachev was awarded the **Nobel Peace Prize** in 1990 for his striking achievements in helping to end the 40-year Cold War.

**Mikhail Gorbachev greets President George Bush**

# 99. Saddam Hussein
## (1937-)

Iraqi dictator **Saddam Hussein's** invasion of Kuwait in 1990 led to the formation of the first post-Cold War U. N. military force and resulted in the **Gulf War**.

Hussein was born into a Muslim peasant family in northern Iraq in 1937. He joined the **Ba'ath Socialist party** in 1957, and participated in several attempts to kill Iraqi prime minister Abdul Kassem. Hussein was imprisoned, but he escaped to Syria and then Egypt when Kassem was overthrown in a coup. Hussein returned to Iraq in 1963, when the Ba'athists briefly took power.

**Saddam Hussein**

By 1968, Hussein had risen to a top position within the Ba'athists, and that year they seized control of Iraq. In 1969, Hussein became deputy chairman of the **Revolutionary Command Council**, the country's new ruling body in the government of Ahmad Hassan al-Bakr.

Hussein became president in 1979 when al-Bakr retired. Hussein quickly focused on strengthening the Iraqi oil industry and gaining a greater foothold in the Arab world. Internally, he used secret police to suppress any opposition to his rule; he also engaged in a brutal repression of the rebellious **Kurdish**

minority, wiping out thousands of Kurds in villages in northern Iraq.

In 1980, Hussein began a bitter war against neighboring Iran to gain control of the Strait of Hormuz. The **Iran-Iraq War** lasted eight years; fought to a stalemate, it ended with a cease-fire agreement in 1988.

Then on August 2, 1990, Hussein sanctioned an Iraqi invasion of neighboring Kuwait. He planned to use that country's oil revenues to bolster Iraq's economy, but the invasion brought about United Nations sanctions. Hussein ignored appeals to withdraw his forces, despite the buildup of a large United States-led multinational military force in Saudi Arabia.

When Hussein refused to relent, the U.N. force attacked on January 16, 1991. In a six-week long war the multinational coalition drove Iraq's armies out of Kuwait. Hussein's troops surrendered in February 1991.

Hussein was immediately confronted with civil war as his army retreated. Shi'ite Muslims and Kurds rebelled, but Hussein put down their uprisings, causing thousands to flee to refugee camps along the country's northern border.

In the aftermath of the Gulf War, a special U.N. delegation was sent to oversee the destruction and removal of all Iraqi nonconventional weapons. Iraq was also prohibited from producing chemical and nuclear weapons. Numerous sanctions were leveled on the country pending compliance, causing severe shortages of food and medicine and further weakening the economy. Initially Iraq refused to disclose all its nuclear sites, but when the allies threatened a resume an air offensive, the Iraqis supplied the necessary information.

In 1995, Hussein held a national referendum and was confirmed as president for seven more years.

# 100. Lech Walesa
(1943– )

A shipyard worker and founder of Poland's first independent trade union, **Lech Walesa** played a major role in ending Communism and bringing about the the rise of democracy in his country.

Walesa was one of eight children born into a worker-peasant family in Popowo, Poland. In 1967, he became an electrician in the **Lenin Shipyards** in Gdansk. In 1970, he participated in the large-scale shipyard demonstrations against the government's decision to increase food prices.

In 1976, Walesa emerged as an antigovernment union activist, and as a result he was fired from his job. In 1980, when workers' strikes once again occurred, Walesa scaled the fence at the Lenin Shipyards to join the workers occupying the site. He took charge of the strike, and negotiated an agreement with the government that gave the workers the right to organize freely and to strike. The shipyard strike influenced workers and farmers throughout Poland.

Walesa then founded the independent trade union *Solidarnosc* (**Solidarity**); in short time, some ten million Polish workers from around the country had registered as members. Walesa's charismatic leadership of Solidarity brought him immediate national and international recognition.

By 1981, worker dissatisfaction and social unrest were increasing, and the Soviet Union was putting pressure on the Polish government to crack down. Defense Minister **Wojciech Jaruzelski** was appointed prime minister, and in December he imposed martial law and outlawed Solidarity. Walesa was arrested, and detained for seven months. For the next six years, he was either under arrest, or watched closely by the secret police. In 1983, he was awarded the **Nobel Peace Prize**, which only angered the Polish government even further.

By December 1988, it was clear that the social unrest and poor economic conditions could not continue. The ruling Communist party invited Walesa to join in negotiations, which lasted for 59 days. In the end, Solidarity was legalized, and the government sanctioned free elections for a limited number of seats in the upper house of the *Sejm* (Parliament). In June 1989, Solidarity won an overwhelming majority of those seats, and after Walesa refused to form a coalition government with the Communists, the Parliament was forced to accept a Solidarity-led government.

In 1990, Walesa ran successfully for president. He then led the country through industrial privatization, and Poland's first set of totally free elections. He also began international relations with the newly emerging states of Central and Eastern Europe, as well as with the Western powers.

Walesa's confrontational style, and his refusal to approve a relaxation of Poland's prohibitions on abortion eroded his popularity late in his term. In 1995, he sought reelection, but was narrowly defeated by the former Communist, **Aleksander Kwasniewski**

**Lech Walesa**

107

# Trivia Quiz & Projects

Test you knowledge and challenge your friends with the following questions. The answers are contained in the biographies noted.

1. Which Babylonian ruler devised a "Code" that governed all aspects of life for his people? (see no. 3)
2. Which ancient Greek statesman led Athens during the height of that city-state's imperial power and cultural greatness? (see no. 8)
3. Who was the ruthless 5th century warrior who led his forces in a series of campaigns that nearly destroyed Western Christendom? (see no. 15)
4. How did a Danish king unite the Danish and English people and become the first person since the fall of Rome to rule all of England? (see no. 23)
5. Which outstanding French ruler consolidated the power of the monarchy and turned his kingdom into a fully organized state? (see no. 28)
6. How did the first woman medieval ruler bring together three Scandinavian countries to form a union that would last for more than 130 years? (see no. 32)
7. Why did a famous Aztec emperor welcome a Spanish conqueror and his army and allow them to capture his capital city and eventually destroy his empire? (see no. 35)
8. Where did an 18th century Russian czar build his new capital to give his country a desired "window to the West"? (see no. 42)
9. Which general transformed the French Revolutionary Republic into an empire and in the process conquered much of Europe? (see no. 48)
10. When did a great Italian patriot lead his armed forces to a victory that unified Italy for the first time since the days of the Roman Empire? (see no. 53)
11. Which U.S. president was unable to convince the senate to approve a treaty and allow the United States to enter the world's first international organization? (see no. 60)
12. What 20th century European agreement became a symbol of appeasement and failed to prevent the outbreak of another world war? (see no. 65)
13. Who served his nation as its leader longer than any other person, and led his country through one of its most turbulent periods in history? (see no. 71)
14. What crisis nearly brought two superpowers to the brink of war? (see no. 80)
15. Why was a U.S. president forced to become the first chief executive to resign his office? (see no. 89)
16. Where did a lawyer turned revolutionary establish the first Communist nation in the Western Hemisphere? (see no. 97)

## Suggested Projects

1. Choose one of the world leaders from this book and write a one page fictional diary entry for one day in that person's life. Pick a day that had some significance for the individual; for example, the day he or she won an important military battle, or the day he or she was awarded the Nobel prize. Or choose a day on which the person met with a severe defeat, or was frustrated in some way by a lack of success. Describe the person's thoughts and feelings with as much detail as you can.

2. Arrange a "meeting" of two of the world leaders in this book who could never have met in real life. Choose two individuals from different eras and perhaps from even different walks of life. (For example, Lorenzo the Magnificent and Napoleon Bonaparte; or Peter the Great and Pope John XXIII.) Imagine what their meeting would be like. Write 1-2 pages describing the scenario of their meeting, and create dialogue between the two leaders. What kinds of questions do you think they would ask each other? Would they approve of the things that each had done in their lifetimes? Be as imaginative as you can.

# Index

Aachen 26
Abbasid dynasty 25, 33
African National Congress
  (ANC) 102
Aix-la-Chapelle, Treaty of
  51
al-Mansur 25
Alaric the Goth 21
Albigensians 34
Alcuin of York 26
Alexander III (pope) 32
Alexander the Great 16,17
Alfred the Great 27
Algeria 83
American Revolution 53,
  54
Anglican Church 43, 46,
  47
Anglo-Saxons 27, 31
Aquino, Corazon 99
Argentina 88, 103
Arianism 23
Aristotle 17, 23
Ark of the Covenant 11
Armenians 76
Arnold of Brescia 32
Arpád dynasty 29
Ashdown, Battle of 27
Aspasia 15
assassination 14, 19, 61,
  95, 97, 98, 99, 101
Atatürk, Kemal 76
Athens 14, 15
atomic bomb 92
Attalus 21
Attila the Hun 22
Austria 50, 51, 62
Austro-Prussian War 62
Ayatollah Khomeini. see
  Hendi, Ruhollah
Aztec Empire 42

Babylon 10, 12, 14
Baghdad 25

Balkan War 76
Balliol, John 38
Bangladesh 98
Bank of the United States
  54
Bannockburn, Battle of 38
Barbarossa. see Frederick I
Bay of Pigs 104
Ben-Gurion, David 80, 89
Berenice 16
Berlin Wall 87, 97, 105
Bismarck, Otto von 62
Blackshirts 79
Boethius 23
Bolívar, Simón 56
Bolshevik party 71, 73, 75,
  87
Bonaparte, Napoléon 55,
  56
Bouvines, Battle of 35
Brazil 64
Bruce, Robert 38
Brutus, Marcus 19
Buddha. see Gautama,
  Siddhartha
Buddhism 13
Burgundians 23
Byzantine Empire 24, 26

Caesar, Julius 16, 19
caliph 25
Camp David Accords 101
canon law 34
Canute the Great 30, 39
Carolingian minuscule 26
Carolingian Renaissance
  26
Cartagena Manifesto 56
Carter, Jimmy 95, 101
Castro, Fidel 97, 104
Catherine the Great 52
Chalons, Battle of 22
Chamberlain, Neville 72,
  74

Charlemagne 26, 28, 32,
  55
Charles V (Holy Roman
  Empire) 44, 45, 46
Chiang Kai-shek 70, 81,
  86
China 18, 70, 81, 86
Christianity 20, 29, 32, 33,
  37, 43
Church of England. see
  Anglican Church
Churchill, Winston 72, 74,
  78, 81
Civil War (U.S.) 61
Clémenceau, Georges 65
Clement III (pope) 32
Cleopatra VII (Egypt) 16
Clovis I (Franks) 23
Code of Hammurabi 10
Cold War 84, 95, 97, 105
Columbus, Christopher 41
common law 31
Communism 70, 73, 75,
  81, 86, 87, 104, 107
Compact of Olney 30
Confucius 18
Congo, Republic of 93
Constantine the Great 20,
  24
Constantinople 20, 24, 34,
  44
Constitutional Convention
  53
Cortéz, Hernán 42, 45
Council of Nicaea 20
courtier 48
Crimean War 63
Crusades 32, 33, 34, 35,
  37
Cuba 87, 97
Cyrus the Great 12, 14

Danes 27, 30, 31
Darius I (Persia) 14

# Index

Darius III (Persia) 17
Dauphin 54
David (Israelite king) 11
Denmark 30, 39
dharma 13
Disraeli, Benjamin 58, 63
Domesday Book 31
Douglas, Stephen 61
Dreyfus, Alfred 65

Edict of Milan 20
Edict of Nantes 48
Edington, Battle of 27
Edward I (England) 38
Egypt 8, 14, 16, 17, 33,
    58, 89, 93, 100, 101
Elizabeth I (England) 47
England 27, 30, 31, 32,
    33, 35, 37, 38, 43, 47,
    58, 63, 68, 72, 74, 103
Enlightenment 50, 51, 52
Ethelred (West Saxons) 27
Ethelred II (England) 30
Ethiopia 85
Eugene III (pope) 32

Falkirk, Battle of 38
Falkland Islands 103
fascism 79, 82, 84, 88
Ferdinand II (Spain) 41,
    45,
First Crusade 33
Florence 40
Four Noble Truths 13
Fourth Crusade 34
Fourth Lateran Council 34
France 35, 48, 54, 55, 62,
    65, 83
Francis I (France) 45
Franco, Francisco 84
Franco-Prussian War 62
Frederick I (Bararossa) 32
Frederick II (Holy Roman

Empire) 35
Frederick the Great
    (Prussia) 50, 51
French Revolution 54, 56

Gandhi, Indira 98
Garibaldi, Giuseppe 60
Gaul 19, 22
Gaulle, Charles de 83
Gautama, Siddhartha 13
Genghis Kahn 36
Germany 28, 32, 62, 72,
    79, 82
Gettysburg Address 61
Ghana 94
Gladstone, William E. 58,
    63
glasnost 105
Godwinsson, Harold 31
Gold Coast. see Ghana
Gorbachev, Mikhail 95,
    103, 105
Goths 21, 23
Great Britain. see England
Great Depression 69, 78
Great Northern War 49
Great Pyramid 8
Greece 14, 15, 17, 21, 69,
    76
gulag 75
Gulf War 106

Hamilton, Alexander 53
Hammarskjöld, Dag 93
Hammurabi 10
Hammurabi's Code 10
Han dynasty 18
Hapsburg-Valois War 46
Hendi, Ruhollah 90
Henry VIII (England) 43,
    46, 47
Herodotus 8
Hirohito 92

Hitler, Adolf 72, 79, 82, 84
Holocaust 80
Holy Roman Empire 28,
    29, 32, 45
Honorius 21
Hsiang Yü 18
Hubertusburg, Treaty of 50
Huguenots 48
Hungary 28
Huns 22
Hussein, Saddam 106

India 98
Indonesia 91
Innocent III (pope) 34
Intermediate Nuclear
    Forces (INF) treaty
    105
Iran 90, 95
Iran-Contra affair 95
Iran-Iraq War 90
Iraq 90, 106
Iron Curtain 74
Isabella I (Spain) 41
Islam 25, 76, 90, 100
Israel 11, 80, 89, 100, 101
Italian Wars 41
Italy 23, 32, 40, 60, 79

Japan 66, 71, 78, 81, 86,
    91, 92
Jefferson, Thomas 53
Jews 23, 37, 41, 58, 65,
    80, 82
John (Lackland) 35, 37
John I (pope) 23
John XII (pope) 28
John XXIII (pope) 77
Juárez, Benito 59
Justinian I 23, 24, 32

kaiser 62
Kao-tsu. see Liu Pang

# Index

Kennedy, John F.  87, 96, 97
Khrushchev, Nikita  87, 97
Khufu  8
Klerk, F. W. de  102
Knights of St. John  44
Knights Templar  33
Korea  66
Kublai Khan  36
Kurds  76, 106
Kuwait, invasion of  106

League of Nations  67, 85
Lechfeld, Battle of  28
Lenin, Vladimir  71, 73, 75
Leo I (pope)  22
Leo VIII (pope)  28
*Lex Talionis*  10
Licinius  20
Liu Pang  18
Lincoln, Abraham  61
Lloyd George, David  68
Lorenzo the Magnificant.
  see Médici, Lorenzo de'
Louis XIV (France)  48
Louis XVI (France)  54
Luther, Martin  43, 45

Macedonia  16, 17
Magna Carta  37
Magyars  28, 29
Malta  44
Mandela, Nelson  102
Mao Tse-tung  70, 81, 86
Marathon, Battle of  14
Marcos, Ferdinand  99
Margaret I (Scandanavia)
  39
Maria Theresa  50, 51, 54
Marie Antionette  54
Martel, Charles  26
Mary I (England)  46, 47
Mary Queen of Scots  47

Maxentius  20
Maximilian (Austria)  59
Médici, Lorenzo de'  40
Meir, Golda  89
Meiji. see Mutsuhito
Mesopotamia  9, 10
Methven, Battle of  38
Mexico  59
Michelangelo  40
Milvian Bridge, Battle of  20
Mongols  36
Monroe Doctrine  59
Montezuma II (Aztec)  42
Moors  41
Munich Agreement  72
Muslims  26, 33, 34, 44,
  76, 99, 101, 106
Mussolini, Benito  79, 84
Mutsuhito  66

Napoleon III (France)  62
Narva, Battle of  49
Nasser, Gamal Abdel  100,
  101
NATO  83
Nazis  72, 77, 82
Nicaea Creed  20
Nicholas II (Russia)  71
Nika riot  24
Nixon, Richard  86, 96, 97
Nkrumah, Kwame  94
Nobel Prize  74, 93, 101,
  102, 105, 107
Northampton, Treaty of  38
Norway  39

Odoacer  23
Organization of African
  Unity (OAU)  85
Ostrogoths  22, 23, 24
Otto II (Brunswick)  35
Otto the Great  28
Ottoman Empire  69, 44

Ottoman Turks  69

Palestine  33, 80, 89
Panama Canal  65
Paris  35
Paris Peace Conference
  65, 67
Pazzi War  40
Pearl Harbor  78, 92
Pedro II (Brazil)  64
Peel, Robert  58
Peloponnesian War  15
*perestroika*  105
Pericles  15
Perón, Juan  88
Persia  12, 14, 17
Peter the Great  49, 52
Pharsalus, Battle of  19
Philip II (Augustus)  32, 33,
  35, 37
Philip II (Macedonia)  17
Philip II (Spain)  46, 47
Philippines  99
Philistines  11
Platea, Battle of  14
Poitiers, Battle of  26
Poland  107
*Pontifex Maximus*  19
Protestant Reformation  45
Protestantism  43, 45, 47
Prussia  50, 51, 62
Ptolemaic dynasty  16
Ptolemy I (Egypt)  16

Rasputin  71
Reagan, Ronald  95, 103,
  105
Redshirts  60
Richard I (Lionhearted)
  (England)  32, 33, 35, 37
Robert I (Bruce) (Scotland)
  38
Robert I (Normandy)  31

111

# Index

Roman Catholic Church 34, 41, 43, 45, 46, 47, 48, 59, 64, 84, 88
Roman Catholic Counter-Reformation 46
Rome, ancient 19, 20, 21
Roncalli, Angelo. see John XXIII (pope)
Roosevelt, Franklin D. 74, 78, 81
Russia 49, 52, 55, 71, 73, 75, 87, 95, 97, 100, 104, 105
Russian Orthodoxy 52, 71
Russo-Japanese War 66, 71

Sadat, Anwar 101
Saladin 33
Salamis, Battle of 14
Sargon the Great 9
satrap 16
Saul 11
Scotland 38
Segni, Lothario de. see Innocent III (pope)
Selassie, Haile 85
Seven Years' War 50, 51
shah 90
Shaka 57
Shakespeare, William 47
Sharpeville Massacre 102
Sikhs 98
Silesia 50, 51
Sino-Japanese War 66
Six-Day War 89, 100
Sixtus IV (pope) 40
slavery 8, 17, 29, 61, 64, 85
Solidarity 107
South Africa 102
Soviet Union. see Russia
Spain 41, 42, 46, 84
Spanish Armada 46, 47

Spanish Civil War 84
Spanish Inquisition 41
Sparta 15
Stalin, Josef 74, 75, 78, 87
Stamford Bridge, Battle of 31
Stephen I 29
Stilicho, Flavius 21
Stirling Bridge, Battle of 38
Suez Canal 58, 93, 100
Sukarno, Achmad 91
Suleiman I (the Magnificent) 44
Sumer 9
Sun Yat-sen 70, 81, 86
Sweden 39
Sweyn I (Denmark) 30

Taiwan (Formosa) 81, 86
Tenochtitlán 42
thanes 27
Thatcher, Margaret 103
Theodora 24
Theodoric the Great 23
Thermopylae, Battle of 14
Third Crusade 32, 33, 35, 37
transubstantiation 34
triumvirate 19
Turkey 69, 76

Umayyad dynasty 25
United Nations 80, 81, 84, 91, 93, 106
United States 53, 60, 61, 78, 84, 95, 96, 97

Vandals 22, 23, 24
Venizélos, Eleutherios 69
Versailles (court of Louis XIV) 48
Versailles, Treaty of 67, 68

Victoria (England) 58, 63, 71
Victorian Age 63
Vietnam War 96
Visigoths 21, 22, 23
vizier 33
Voltaire 50, 52

Walesa, Lech 107
War of the Austrian Succession 50, 51
War of the Spanish Succession 48
Washington, George 53
Watergate scandal 96
Waterloo, Battle of 55
Wedmore, Treaty of 27
Wessex 27
William the Conqueror 31
Wilson, Woodrow 65, 67
witan 31
World Council of Churches 77
World War I 65, 67, 68, 69, 73, 76, 77, 79, 80, 82
World War II 72, 74, 78, 79, 81, 82, 83, 84, 92

Xerxes I (Persia) 14, 17

Yalta Conference 74, 75, 78
Yom Kippur War 89, 101

Zeno 23
ziggurat 14
Zionism 80, 89
Zulu Empire 57
Zulu War 57